The Underground Shopper

The Underground Shopper

PUBLISHER, EDITOR-IN-CHIEF AND FULL TIME PRINCESS/ susan goldstein

MANAGING EDITOR AND FORMER ADVANCE MAN FOR CIRCUSES, CARNIVALS AND WANDA, THE BEARDED LADY/ bruce mcdougal

RESEARCH MARVELS/ linda conner
alisanne frew,

WRITERS, POETS AND VARIOUS OTHER STRANGE PERSONS/ elaine goode
john hilburn
wendy blum
pam shaw
richard dosher

PROMOTIONAL STUNTMEN/ planned tv arts, nyc
rick frishman
mike levine

COVER DESIGN/ john nieto

PRODUCTION PRIESTESS/ loi bradburry

COMPTROLLER OF THE UNCOMPTROLLABLE/ betty harris

SUE'S PHOTO/ mary ann sherman

SUE'S MAKEUP/ camille freitas

SUE'S GOLD NAIL/ the nailery, dallas

TYPESETTER/ janet wahl

HYPOS AND TYPOS/ linda boyce
cindy edens

BATHROOM TISSUE/ any cheap, house brand

ISBN 0-934180-01-6

Dedicated to short people
in general,
but most particularly to Josh,
whose smallness is only temporary
but whose capacity to love
in huge amounts
will go on forever.

WHY SOME MERCHANTS WOULD HAVE MORE LUCK GETTING A REAL STAR THAN ONE OF OURS.

RATING CODES		CREDIT CODES	
		$	Cash preferred
****	Our favorite	CK	Checks accepted
***	Excellent	AE	American Express
**	Very good	CB	Carte Blanche
*	Worth a trip	DC	Diner's Club
NO STAR	Draw your own conclusions	MC	Master Charge
NV	Not visited	SC	Shopper's Charge
NR	Not rated	V	Visa

Wherever the code NR (Not Rated) appears, it means either that the store was not open for business at the time of our visit, the information arrived too late to meet our deadline, or the featured merchandise was difficult to rate by comparison. For the sake of fairness, periodic sales were not rated; nor were any services. There is no negative connotation attached to NR.

HOW WE RATE THEM. HOW YOU CAN, TOO.

Each judgment of the members of our shopping research team is based on comprehensive adherence to an established rating guideline, as well as our own personal observations. We don't give points for the 8 grand they spent wrapping aluminum foil around the ceiling support posts. Or for their front row center seat in The Galleria. Or for the two page ad they run every other day. Somebody has to pay for all that, and we try to see that it isn't you.

We do give points in eleven major categories, the most important of which are:

— Quality:	The best or the worst; is this a dumping ground for past years' faddish flops, or is the merchandise current?
— Selection:	Would more than one customer in the store at the same time be apt to cause a fight over availability, or is there plenty of a good thing?
— Prices:	We don't want the proprietor to end up in the poor house, but we aren't interested in paying the rent on his penthouse, either.
— Sales Personnel:	Condescending, patronizing and pushy? Or glad you're there and willing to show it.
— Credit Availability:	Cash, plastic or Type "O".

Merchants also get points for cleverness, when that ingenuity saves you money. An easily accessible location where the rent is reasonable, is a plus. Stocking merchandise we know to be good stuff is another.

We want to be treated as customers and not as an interruption of the store clerk's backgammon tournament. Sales personnel who are helpful, informative and willing to let us take our time win points. A clerk who dares to ask, "Can I help you, HONEY?" is immediately down for the count.

We also examine the merchant's return policy—"Glad to see ya' " or "Mad to beat ya'." We don't overlook such amenities as a clothing store's dressing facilities; points off if we have to try on in full view of the sales personnel, other customers and the man who reads the gas meter.

Summing up, the closer a place gets to the optimum of really low prices on high quality goods, sold in a friendly, helpful manner, the closer to 4 stars it will be.

(I HOPE WE'RE NOT BEING) FOREWORD:

Over two million cheapskates can't be wrong. In every city where **THE UNDERGROUND SHOPPER** is published, it has made the best seller list. From New York to San Antonio, from Houston to Detroit, our bargain guides are big hits with Mrs. (and Ms. and Mr.).

Thousands of Houstonians, new and old, have discovered we are the classy alternative to old Demon Markups. They found it's no more a privilege to purchase from the posh than it would have been an honor to be a galley slave on Cleopatra's barge.

This book is divided into two sections. In the first half of the book are the NEW listings. As usual, we haggled and bargained, lost our innocence in community dressing rooms and trekked through enough dusty warehouses to write a thesis on brown lung.

The second half lists all our old, tried-and-true (and a few tried-and-boo) outlets. Most are stores that have consistently offered exceptional bargains to help inflation-ravaged budgets. The information about these shops has been updated by phone and personal visit.

Please take note of our neat, new "Mail Order" section in the back of the book. From cigars to tools, big money can be saved postally.

Take heart, Houston! With **THE UNDERGROUND SHOPPER,** you can live high on the hog at macaroni prices!

ACKNOWLEDGEMENTS: Abundant appreciation to my office and production staff, who rescued, raved, ranted and reviewed with regularity. Heartfelt thanks to the shoppers who fizzled after the first hot warehouse, and to the others who didn't; to Alisanne Frew, who flew in and out of every last shop and literally saved more than the day. Special thanks to Richard, who drove us everywhere but crazy. A nod of appreciation to Quality Olds in McKinney, Texas, for being the absolute best car dealer we've been able to find. Thank you, John, for your profundity, puns and cheap housing. Much gratitude to the many media friends who support our efforts; to merchants who continue to live up to their ratings; to Rusty, whose dream of isles, I treasure, too. And to my folks, who raised me to be an above ground princess, my love.

SIBLING RIFLERY: Wendy Dunn is always on target. She is a straight shooter—the wittiest, wildest, most wonderful sister in the world. At current market quotes, her heart should fetch $300 per troy ounce. Many thanks for her incalculably valuable assistance. For all of you who don't have a brother-in-law in the business, I can only wish for you a sister like mine.

NON-ACKNOWLEDGEMENTS: To those of you with whom I have associated, who would have, in other times:

- Sold matches and firewood in old Salem.

- Parked your rich grandmother's wheelchair beside a tall building during the San Francisco earthquake.

- Peddled German language roadmaps of North Africa to Erwin Rommel in 1942.

- Had Ben Franklin committed because of his peculiar obsession with kites.

My wish is that you should all spend a lively week at Club Med . . . together.

SUE GOLDSTEIN, PUBLISHER

Distributed in the Houston area by:

EAST TEXAS PERIODICALS
7171 Grand Boulevard
Houston, Texas 77054
(713) 748-8120

TABLE OF CONTENTS

NEW LISTINGS SECTION

AD ALTERNATIVES

****
GREEN SHEET
7701 Allen Parkway
Houston
Tel. 526-6841

No news is good news. We found the Green Sheet to be 100% advertising, free to its readers. Claimed to be the largest weekly circulation in Texas. It was found in drug, grocery, convenience and other stores. Personal ads were .25/word, and business or service ads were $10.90/column inch. Paper came out on different days in different areas of Houston. CK

ANTIQUES

**
ANTIQUE CO-OP
1430 Gessner
Houston
Tel. 932-6986
Sun-S 10-5:30

It's a cheaper buy, due to the dozen here. The twelve dealers we saw in one building (and five more next door) cooperate in the antique business. We discovered a small chest for $175—a good price for similar quality we had seen elsewhere. Dr. Discount says never get a new chest when an old one will do! We also found a small, oak, roll top desk ($1000), milk cans ($15-$17) and lots of trays ($6.50). If you know your prices before you go, you may find some real bargains. CK

**
THE ANTIQUE KEY
1427 Gessner
Houston
Tel. 461-2524
T-Sun 10-5

Great Scott, Francis, this Key is an expert on antique locks. They specialize in fitting keys to antique locks. Prices seemed a little high, but the owner was very knowledgeable, interesting and informative. He wasn't keyed up at all when talking about his clocks ($50). They repair old tickers, too. Also found lots of furniture like small chests ($325), pot stands ($50-$60). Their bric will lead us brac again. CK, MC, SC, V

**
**CRAWFORDS
TRADING POST**
Hwy. 149
Tomball
Tel. 259-7459
Sun-S 11-4

If you believe the hunt is half the thrill, check out Crawford's. They have more buried treasure than Long John Silver ever dreamed about. This dirty, dark, dank but delightful old house was full of junk. B.Y.O. flashlight; they'll supply the mixes of glasswares, tools, furniture, clothing or whatever. B.Y.O. junk and they'll trade, too. CK

8

Pots, plant stands and primitive pine pieces were among the highlights in Davenport & Co., an exquisitely reasonable shop full of antiques and collectibles. We didn't want to step over the great assortment of Oriental rugs (and we don't mean Charlie Chan's toupee). We saw lots of bamboo, but few bamboo-boos. The overall discounts averaged about 30% under what comparable merchandise was going for in other establishments. Judy, Lydia and Sandy were the delightful partners who minded the store (watch out for the readhead). CK

****
DAVENPORT & CO.
1653 Blalock
Houston
Tel. 461-7775
M-S 9-5:30

We're not just a'wolfin' when we say Grannies had a big selection. Handmade quilts, dolls, pillows, pottery, baskets, enamelware and stoneware (but nary a riding hood) were all the better (goodies) to have seen her with. Prices were good on some items, high on others. We figured an average 10-15% discount. Granny, we ate up the yard eggs we saw at .86 per dozen. Look for the old house with the EGGS sign on the door. CK

*
GRANNIES GOODIES
11020 Timberline
Houston
Tel. 465-0525
T-S 10-4

Little's things mean a lot (but they don't cost a bunch). We rate their prices at the very reasonable level. The outside of the building looked like Judge Roy Beans' summer house. Inside, we found displays on walls, beds, chests and shelves. We saw someone just like your grandmother, sitting in a rocker. She acknowledged our arrival and invited us to "Help ourselves, look around, and if you need anything, holler". We discovered beautiful old quilts ($120), a gilded gold mahogany frame and mirror ($225) and antique wardrobes ($225 up). Loads of antique furniture, books, linens, handkerchiefs, depression glass and jewelry. Don't go in unless the gate is open. Little's doberman is BIG. CK, SC

***
**LITTLE'S ANTIQUES
& COUNTRY JUNK**
1246 Wirt Road
Houston
Tel. 686-2761
M-F 10-4/S by appt.

This house made us pine for the good, old days (when prices were low). Their quality was excellent, but not a bargain. Most antiques were made of pine, like the beautiful dry sink at $695. Small accessories were .50 up. CK

*
PINE HOUSE ANTIQUES
9035 Lariat
Houston
Tel. 461-1621
T-S 10-5

**

R & F ANTIQUES
411 Washington
Houston
Tel. 861-7750
M-S 10-5

We found beds of wrought iron ($275) and brass ($1200) that would last even if we lived to be as old as Methuselah. The owner had been very selective in his purchases. This was not a junk store. Considering the quality, we thought the prices were reasonable on an oak rocking chair ($295), wicker chairs ($225), wooden file cabinets ($300), ice boxes in mint condition ($395) and an old wall card cabinet for collector items ($450). Also saw milk cans and old claw footed bathtubs. Friendly folks. MC, V

**

**STOP 'N SAVE
ANTIQUES**
2125 Bingle
Houston
Tel. 461-3424
M-S 9:30-6:30

We were glad to see that their merchandise showed more imagination than their store name. The prices were good considering the excellent quality we found. We saw a six hook oak hall tree with original mirror and finish in mint condition ($175) and a refinished, upholstered morris chair ($275). Successful family operation, located in small building in front of home. They will not dicker. MC, V

ANTIQUES: REPAIRS

*BISSONNET
ANTIQUES*
4817 Bissonnet
Houston
Tel. 666-5336
T-S 9-5

These people were proud, but would strip for the public at token prices. We caught their act with kitchen chairs ($10-$50), a buffet ($35-$50) and a china cabinet ($40-$50). Prices higher for stubborn paint. Saw New England antiques and stained and beveled glass, for those who like higher class performances. CK, MC, V

*MEMORIAL POLISH-
ING AND PLATING
COMPANY*
9061 Gaylord
Houston
Tel. 464-1429
M-F 8:30-5/S 10:30-2

We took a shine to Memorial. Mr. Goodman, the owner, specialized in polishing and plating. He also had a reasonably priced selection of brass, bronze and silver artifacts. We reflected upon beautiful, antique, English brass mirrors, brass flower pots ($32.50) and a 30" solid brass tray ($100). He had antique-painted, children's banks for $21.50 ($40 elsewhere). CK, V

Confucious say, "Settler who is hit in head by lemon meringue have pie-on-ear." These old settlers slap sticks with their complete line of removers, refinishers, polishes, stains and varnishes. Top labels like BURNETT, MENNEX and CONSTANTINE. The all female personnel possessed a highly polished knowledge of products that we found to be very helpful. They had a few antique gifts scattered throughout the shop. The large spinning wheel ($275) was woven-derful. We "finished" our shopping and varnished out the door. MC

THE SETTLERS
1437 W. Alabama St.
Houston
Tel. 524-2417
T-S 10-6

APARTMENT LOCATORS

One thing is certain; the price is right. It's free. Home in on these locators if you're through housing around. Excellent service for those in a hurry or those who don't know their way around town. Their resources are not infinite, so it is possible you may not hear about many of the apartments in Houston. It is also a wise thing to remember that many apartment houses are not affiliated with locator services because they don't have to be. FREE

APARTMENT
LOCATING CENTER
3001-K Fondren
Houston
Tel. 784-1722
M-F 9-5/S 10-2

APPAREL: CHILDREN'S

Chocolate Soup grows on you. They have a dozen locations now, and it looks like they will continue to expand. They sell children's clothes (from goo-goo's to young teens) direct from the factory. We found LONDON FOG jackets ($37.50) and coats ($79.95), jumpers at half price ($13-$25), shorts ($7.75 up) and dresses ($13 up). Saw cute purses and novelty items scattered throughout. They also did monograming. CK, MC, V

**
CHOCOLATE SOUP
12850 Memorial Drive
Houston
Tel. 467-5957
M-S 10-5:30

11

APPAREL: FAMILY

***

THE INLOOK OUTLET
8415 Stella Link
Houston
Tel. 668-7210
M-S 9:30-6

The Inlook Outlet outlook is for lotsa bargains at great prices. Their policy is to give 50% off and we wouldn't argue much with that. Men's and women's clothes and some fabric. We spotted some great men's sport shirts for $7.95-$9.95. MC, V

NR

LILLY PULITZER
1706 S. Post Oak
Houston
Tel. 627-8150
M-S 9:30-5:30

It would never be necessary to gild this Lilly. She is too elegant. She received critical praise from us for her novel, hand-screened, poly-cotton prints ($8/yd.), patchworks ($15/yd.), ready-made dresses ($74-$82), blouses ($40), slacks ($58), bibs ($5.50) and children's robes ($15). She made clothes to fit infants to senior citizens. But the real story was the racks of material covering the walls. CK, MC, V

****

WEARHOUSE NO. 18
9824 Harwin
Houston
Tel. 783-2810
T-Sun 10-6

The best little Wearhouse in Texas. How about VERA blouses for $6.99 (reg. $21) and ACT III for $16.99 (reg. $38)? GANT forget men's clothing, either. We found GANT and PIERRE CARDIN shirts for $14.99. Stocked mainly for women, however. Discounts were 45-75% storewide, but had to sift through a lot of not-so-hot stuff to find the good stock. Located in a warehouse area, back off the road, The Wearhouse is a little hard to find. It's worth the effort, though. $

APPAREL: MEN'S

**

HIS PLACE
13162 Memorial Drive
Houston
Tel. 932-1485
M-S 10-6

Tell your man to stay in His Place (if you want to save about 25% on men's clothing). His clothing was first quality—labels like ARROW, VAN HEUSEN and HAGGAR. Saw shirts from $6.99-$11.99 (reg. $13-$15) and sports coats at $42 (reg. $60). CK, MC, V

APPAREL: WOMEN'S

Crazy like a fox. And if foxy is how you want to look, head down Sage Road to Crazy Joe's. Designer merchandise at 30-60% off convinced us Joe is not cuckoo at all! We saw GIVENCHY sport knit separates for $26.99 (reg. $48), RALPH LAUREN skirts for $39 (reg. $69), ANNE KLEIN cashmere sweaters at $89.99 (reg. $140), ST. MARTINE velour shirts at $19.99 (reg. $22) and ST. GERMAINE 100% silk dresses for $74.99 (reg. $98). Store was very nice with well-mannered (sane) personnel. CK, MC, V

****
CRAZY JOE'S
2680 Sage Road
Houston
Tel. 965-0574
M-S 10-6

Disc-o-mode is stopped up (with bargains)! Discotheque a look at some of the dance floor hits at this shop. Jeans from $28-$35 were marked down to $18-$21. Dresses from $45-$60 were marked down to $18-$38. We saw 25-50% discounts throughout, but European designs they weren't. Maybe COCO OF CALIFORNIA or JUST FOR YOU are the newest steps to fashion supremacy. Worth a trip. Other location at 7551 Westheimer. CK, MC, V

**
DISC-O-MODE
1029 Gessner
Houston
Tel. 465-8410
M-F 10-8/S 10-6

What's a WIGGLE WORM doing in a Fashion Center? It's good bait to introduce 30-60% savings on women's clothes in the large sale area of the store. You may come in grub-by, but you can leave with a LORCH suit at 50% off. Lots of co-ordinates, pants, suits and skirts from folks like ALEX COLEMAN and SOUTH SEAS. Sizes from 6-20 with moderate prices overall. CK, MC, V

**
FASHION CENTER
10932 Westheimer
Houston
Tel. 784-2540
M-S 10-6

Finder here and keeper happy. The weeping losers are the ones who didn't know about their women's designer clothes at super savings (at least 1/3 off). DONKENNY pants were on sale the day we visited for $5 (reg. $13-$19). CALVIN KLEIN pants and jeans were $28, DEJA-VU tops (where in the world did we see those before?) $4, beautiful sweaters were $12-$14 (reg. $24-$38) and fashionable swimsuits were going for $5-$9. Saw other designer clothes by GLORIA VANDERBILT, YSL, BILL BLASS, COCONUTS, AMANDA and CIAO. Sold juniors and misses in sizes 3-16. The selection was outstanding. CK, AE, MC, SC, V

****
FINDERS KEEPERS
11188 Fondren
Houston
Tel. 981-4116
M-F 10-9/S 10-6

13

***

JEANS & DREAMS
6839 S. Gessner
Houston
Tel. 981-9506
M-T 10-6/W-Th 10-7
F 10-8/S 10-6

"Doctor, I dreamed I fell from a plane. I crashed through a store's roof and landed on a waterbed, which bounced me onto a rack of designer jeans. What does it all mean?" "Dot vas no nightmare! You vas in Jeans And Dreams!" Sure enough, their jeans were a dream come true. We found WILD OATS, FADED GLORY and JORDACH racked at $10 (reg. $18-$30). Furthermore, if you floated a loan for $99.95, you could get a water-ful deal on a NEW WORLD waterbed. We found the combination of denim trousers and liquid beds unusual AND profitable. CK, MC, V

****

KINDA KRAZY
13192 Memorial Drive
Houston
Tel. 464-3024
M-S 10-6/Th 10-8

The decor was bright orange, but even a dyed in the wool Aggie would be unable to resist their fantastic bargains on women's sportswear and coordinated casuals. We found 30-60% savings on BOBBI BROOKS, ALEX COLEMAN and BODIN. They also carried ROSANNA, Danna. It would be Kinda Krazy not to shop them for swimwear, too. They had an enormous selection of JANTZEN wear (you'll love it, David). We saw BOBBI BROOKS slacks ($14-$17.50), ALEX COLEMAN slacks and blouses ($13-$17), ALEX COLEMAN jackets ($25-$30) and JANTZEN bathing suits were $6-$19 (reg. $20-$35). Personnel were all models of helpfulness. Check other locations: 7435 S.W. Freeway at Fondren, 2352 FM 1960 W., 19645 Eastex Freeway, Humble and 21953 E. Katy Freeway in Katy. CK, MC, V

**

**PAULINES
SPORTSWEAR**
7221½ Bissonnet
Houston
Tel. 777-3331
M-F 9-6/S 9:30-5:30

I asked my little sister if she knew about Pauline's. She said, "Yes, I buy one everytime I eat at a Mexican restaurant!" She was close. The bargains on sportswear and accessories were something to sink your teeth into. Saw a sale rack with 40-75% off on dresses, blouses, pantsuits and gabardine skirted suits. Brands like COS COB, SHIP 'N' SHORE and ALADDIN and COLE. Dresses were at least 20% off all the time. There was a big selection of currently styled merchandise. CK, MC, SC, V

Are you unsuitable? We found 20-30% off on lined, poly-blend suits (some with pants). Working out of her residence, this lady captured the styles—the latest versions of slits and flares, in a nicely tailored look. Prices started at $48 and went up from there. $

*
SUITS
Houston
Tel. 444-4062
Call for appt.

You can really go to Towne there. Top designers like GIVENCHY, GEOFFREY BEENE, GLORIA VANDERBILT and OSCAR DE LA RENTA were present, at around 50% off. We found a good selection of jeans for $17.95 and a few suits at $80 (reg. $190), but they were like needles in a haystack. Sizes were from 3-16. About jumped out of our Gucci's when we heard that infamous phrase, "Can I help you, Honey?" from one of the sales clerks! We wouldn't call them snobby, but . . . CK, MC, V

**
TOWNE SHOP
3200 Richmond
Houston
Tel. 524-1079
Call for hours

MISS SHAHEEN, DURELL, MELISSA LANE and LORCH are out of their wardrobe and into ours, thanks to the 20-50% discounts we found. We loved the large selection of OLGA and VASSARETTE bras at $3.50 (reg. $6 up) and HANES pantyhose for $1 (reg. $1.65). We felt the quality of their dresses was not 100% great. A careful, selective shopper could have a ball in The Wardrobe. CK, MC, V

**
THE WARDROBE
2240 W. Holcombe
Houston
Tel. 668-3949
M, S 9:30-5:30
T-F 9:30-6

APPLIANCES

This M & M melted the competition. Prices were very low on SCOTCH blank tapes: one hour Beta ($9.95), two hour VHS ($14.95), two hour Beta ($12.95) and four hour VHS ($17.50). They also had full length features like "Cleopatra", "Patton", "The African Queen" and many, many more. Admission prices ranged from $49.95-$74.95. CK, MC, V

****
M & M VIDEO
SYSTEMS INC.
4401 S. Main St.
Houston
Tel. 523-6369
M-S 8-8

APPLIANCES

****
**HOUSTON
CONSUMER CENTER**

See write-up under "Buying Services."

**
**PROVEN PRODUCTS
CO.**
8931 Gulf Freeway
Houston
Tel. 943-3870
M-F 8-5/Th 8-9/S 8-3

Wash away your appliance woes by cooking up a Proven deal here. All major brands like HOTPOINT, WHIRLPOOL, AMANA, MAYTAG, JENN AIR, FRIGIDAIRE, etc. We loved the WHIRLPOOL washer/dryer combination for $498. Their service was quite good. They've been in business 28 years and have liberal credit terms. Try other location at Miramar Center. CK

**NR
RALPH'S APPLIANCE**
Houston
Tel. 463-7835
Call for appt.

Ralph's deals are close to wholesale, and they ought to be. Talk about low overhead! They operate out of their home, stock nothing and order goods specifically for their customers. Ralph says "shop for your appliance, get the brand, model number and price and we'll beat it". Ralph didn't explain what happens if our appliance breaks down. CK

ART

*
FRENCH GALLERY
11684 S.W. Fwy.
Houston
Tel. 498-1604
T-S 10-5

Lafayette, we've had enough! They had de Gaulle to offer original oil paintings ($7.50 up) that appeared to have been done by les enfants terrible. The more expensive pictures were considerably better. Small unfinished frames were $2.50 (8 X 10) and larger ones were $3 (12 X 16). Compared to many other galleries, the prices here were fair to good. Worth a trip. MC, SC, V

**NR
SPEEDBYS OLD
PRINTER**
5017 Montrose
Houston
Tel. 521-9652
T-S 11-3

Don't speed by. It takes time to appreciate the loads of 16th-20th century American, British and European artworks. Unusual collection of prints, postcards, greeting cards, maps, wood cuts, drawings (and more) from $1-$300. Tiny store filled with the Edwardian and Victorian collections of Elsa Ross. Located on Montrose near the Fine Arts Museum. CK

AUCTIONS

Peek in Bekins. You'll be moved to bid on the loads of unclaimed freight. Bekins unloads their autumn auction in late October or early November. Call to secure the dates. Watch for experienced bidders (the place is a stomping ground for pros) so you'll know how to bid. Best to go early and stay late so as not to miss the good-byes. CK

NR
BEKINS MOVING & STORAGE (AUCTION)
3502 Bissonnet
Houston
Tel. 988-1200
Late October-Early November

Ever wonder where you can find the best deal on dishes from the China seize? Merchandise from around the world that has been grabbed by U.S. Customs is sold to the public once a year in Houston. It's the custom for people to attend from all parts of the States for this one. It's hard to find a treasure, because bids can go high. Sure is fun to try, though. $

NR
CUSTOMS AUCTION
U. S. Government
Houston
Tel. 921-5136
        226-4314
Usually in November

A real, class act. They are the Oveta Culp Hobby of the auction business. Established firmly and famously in London, New York and Los Angeles, they now have a branch in the Galleria (third level). Many items are biggies, but 75% are less than $1000. Attendance is like taking an ancient history lesson (and a course in Economics). $

NR
SOTHEBY PARKE-BERNET INC.
The Galleria
Third Level
Tel. 623-0010
Call for hours

T.G.I.A.N. (Thank Goodness It's Auction Night). Every Friday night (sometimes Saturday) they hold an antique auction. Sales are different every week. One week it might be a sale of primitives. Next week might see an auction featuring depression glass or the liquidation of an estate. A QUEEN ANNE china cabinet caught our auc-ten-tion when we visited. Prices seemed quite reasonable. CK

**
SPRING BRANCH AUCTION GALLERY
1717 Campbell Road
Houston
Tel. 464-1055
F, some S
Auctions start at 7 p.m.

AUTOMOTIVE

NR
AUTOMOBILE
AUCTION
5711 Eastex Fwy.
Houston
Tel. 222-3250
Periodic Sales 8-3:30

The auto-thorities of Houston have an auction twice a year (usually spring and fall), where they foist off around 600 surplus and unclaimed automobiles. There are some excellent buys, but don't expect help from the Department of Consumer Affairs if your clunker clunks out. $

AUTOPATCH, INC.
2111 Marnel
Houston
Tel. 467-5851
M-F 8-6

You say your beetle has been squashed? See Dale Shanks (owner) for an estimate on body repair. Their specialties are partial and new paint jobs, fender and fiberglass work on small American and foreign cars. They didn't steer us wrong—very honest and factual. MC, V

CARSHARE
Houston
Tel. 227-0003
M-F 8-5

CARSHARE!! God bless you! Runny nose or not, you're better off sharing your misery in a car pool. Get out of the gas lines and into the wonderful world of gang commuting. Applications are accepted by phone. Give home address and zip code, work address, work hours, work number and whether you want to ride or drive or both. Your application is computer processed and matched with your nearest common denominator. This free service is sponsored by the Mass Transit Association. FREE

GESSNER AUTO
SALES
1902 Gessner
Houston
Tel. 461-4496
M-F 9-6/S 9-4

You auto "rent a wreck" from here if your chugger is in the shop. Used cars rented for $14/day or $80/week with no mileage charge. We wreckcon that's a good deal. New car rates were $18/day or $100/week. They required a 2 day minimum and $100 deposit when we trucked by. Insurance is your problem. CK, MC, V

NR
HOUSTON AUTO
AUCTION (USED)
2436 Bissonnet
Houston
Tel. 523-2786
M-F 8-5
Auction every 2 weeks

If you have LOTS of guts, this is a good way to buy a car. At Houston Auto Auction, you can buy and sell trucks, vans, cars and equipment at dealer prices. No guarantees, folks. If you're selling a car, take it in the Monday before the auction. Usually get the same price as a trade in. If you're purchasing, get there around 9 a.m. to get a bidder number. If you buy, there is a $15 charge. CK

See write-up under "Buying Services."

They deal in "hot" cars (the kinds with broken air conditioners). Sonny and Bill work only on automatic transmissions and air conditioning, and beat dealership prices by a country mile. They are honest and reputable and they don't try to take advantage of you or your car. Garage sets well off the road, so look for their sign. MC, V

Is your car desperate for a "fix?" Let George do it. George (owner) is an auto mechanic. He takes special pains with non-mechanical ladies, and explains in laywoman's terms what is wrong with their auto. Good prices. All work guaranteed. CK

****
**HOUSTON
CONSUMER CENTER**

SONNY'S
AUTOMATIC TRANS-
MISSION & AIR
CONDITIONING
SERVICE
1544 Campbell Road
Houston
Tel. 468-0741
M-F 8-6

SPRING BRANCH
GARAGE
1544 Campbell Road
Houston
Tel. 465-5666
M-F 8-6

BEAUTY

If it takes cosmetic surgery to cut enough cash loose from your husband to pay for your beauty aids, you need a Beautiful Visions Catalog. 50% (and better) savings on such names as POLLY BERGEN (lipsticks for .95, TORTUE spray mist for $2.50), COTY (Sweet Earth suds or mud—.50), MAX FACTOR (lip gloss for .95) and HELENA RUBENSTEIN (nail color for .85). Plus much, much more. Write for catalog.

****
**BEAUTIFUL VISIONS
102 Marcus Drive
Melville, NY 11746**

Send for their free fragrance cards, and sample 42 famous smells. Their price for ½ oz. of copy perfume is $5.75, compared to as much as $175/oz. for the real McCoy.

****
**ESSENTIAL
PRODUCTS CO. INC.
90 Water Street
New York, NY 10005**

This is a Perfumery. "Jerry" made perfumed copies of all the popular fragrances at savings of up to 80%. They are produced under the TOUCH & GO label. All fragrances are numbered. ESTEE LAUDER'S Youth Dew is No. 3. Opium is No. 50. The scents are 100% pure concentrated fragrance, not 90% alcohol! They last about 3 months. Send for their catalogue. You'll love it.

****
**HOUSE OF
INTERNATIONAL
FRAGRANCES
4711 Blanco Rd.
San Antonio, TX 78212**

BICYCLES

NR
BIKE SALE
5711 Eastex Frwy.
Houston
Tel. 222-3250
8 a.m./2nd working
day of the month

You have to get geared up early for this one, or you'll miss it. The sale starts at 8 a.m. and all the bikes are usually sold within 30 minutes. The City of Houston Treasury Department sponsors the sale of unclaimed, lost or stolen bikes obtained from the Police Department. The second working day of every month. They pedal 50 to 75 bikes at prices from around $5-$35. $

NV
HOUSTON
BICYCLE CO.
2207 Commonwealth
Houston
Tel. 522-1852
T-F 12-6/S 10-4

Who ever thought a man named "Bentley" would have it in for automobiles? Joe Bentley gave up driving cars long ago, but he does deal in wheels. He operates a bicycle repair shop, sells new and used bikes and hands out advice to other bike enthusiasts. We hear his service is excellent. We didn't get a chance to visit Joe before press. Our bike had a flat. $

HOUSTON BIKE
CENTER, INC.
11188 Fondren
Houston
Tel. 777-6660
M-F 10-7/S 10-6

Bike prices here made us want to take a hike, but service has been spoken of highly. They sold RALEIGH bikes and mopeds at full retail. Their service rode well with us, however. A total bike check up was $18 plus parts, and all repair costs were clearly posted. Dependable work. CK

****
HOUSTON
CONSUMER CENTER

See write-up under "Buying Services."

BOOKS

**
BOOK CENTER
1030 Gessner
Houston
Tel. 465-2907
M-S 10-6

My sister just finished "Scruples." She said the book sent'er. This Book Center will, too. Everything from comics to classics, with prices from .10 up. Used and new books. Books were shelved according to author and subject. Buy a book, read it, then sell it back. Check directory for other locations. CK

Brandeis is one of our favorite book sales. It takes place once a year and usually offers around 30,000 books for sale. Prices range from .25 for paperbacks to $6 for collector's items. All donated, tax-deductible books will be picked up on request by local alums. Profits go to the Brandeis Library, and unsold books go to various charities. CK

NR
BRANDEIS
UNIVERSITY
WOMEN'S
COMMITTEE BOOK
SALE
Sharpstown Shop. Ctr.
Houston
Tel. 623-0490
Call for hours

Jane looks for exchange, students. If you've two digested paperbacks sitting in the corner, trade them for one you haven't read. Discounting the trade theory, used paperbacks were discounted 50% off list. Large selections of best sellers, non-fiction, mysteries, sci-fi and comics. She also buys and trades stamps and cigarette coupons (cough!). CK

* * *
JANE'S PAPERBACK
BOOK & TRADING
STAMP EXCHANGE
6063 Bissonnet
Houston
Tel. 668-8892
M-S 10-5:30

Make this place a Hobbit even if you've only a Tolkien interest in science fiction and fantasy. We saw books by George Orwell, Richard Adams and Isaac Asimov. We exhumed games, prints, maps and poster movie stills of classics like "The Bride of Frankenstein" and "The Werewolf of London" ($2.50-$5.95). Used books were $1 up. We looked for Cousin Ralph's new book. It's about a famous actress who started out as a lady of the evening. It's called "Star Trick." They had never heard of it. CK

NR
OTHER WORLDS
BOOKSTORE
2309 University
Houston
Tel. 665-1714
W-Sun 10-7

A dog-eared delight! P & M will exchange used paperbacks and magazines on a two for one basis plus a 20% charge. $

*
PAPERBACK &
MAGAZINE
EXCHANGE
10722 FM 1960 W
Houston
Tel. 469-7820
M-F 11-7/S 10-5

**NR
CHELSEA
DECORATIVE
METAL CO.**
1302 Peden St.
Houston
Tel. 524-7719
Call for appt.

Aunt Myrtle spent eight years in the Army, building barracks. She was assigned to the ceiling WACS. She never turned out work as beautiful as Chelsea, however. We discovered their ceilings were reproductions of old-time metal ones. They had 18 designs plus nine border trims from which to choose. Average price was $1.50/sq. ft. Mail orders accepted and can ship statewide. Free catalogue available. CK

****
PROKOP LUMBER**
14105 South Post Oak
Houston
Tel. 433-4545
M-F 8-5:30/S 8-4:30

Have you been thinking of building on and living happily ever rafter? Then lumber on in. We found plywood $1-$2 cheaper per sheet than some we priced elsewhere, insulation .01/sq. ft. less and sheetrock about .40 per sheet cheaper. They also had good deals on paint, floor covering, roofing, fencing and paneling. Lumber wasn't discounted much as far as we could tell. Their claim is that they are the king of the discounters. Less regal, we believe. CK, MC, V

****
SAN JACINTO
SALES CO.**
2327 Ann St.
Houston
Tel. 225-1131
M-S 7:30-5

It would probably be a monumental mistake not to buy some of your home improvement needs here. Their corrugated steel sheets, fencing, pipes, septic tanks ($99.95) and 6 cu. ft. wheel barrows ($69.95) were priced inside the ballpark. We thought the service was a little ragged, but they were very busy. MC, V

*****
SUTHERLAND
LUMBER**
7502 Washington
Houston
Tel. 869-4611
M-F 8-9/S 8-5

"Donald, Sutherland was great!" We found that if you need a wheel barrow ($14.95), a post hole digger ($6.95) or half a whisky barrel ($11.75), Sutherland was a good place to get them. We spotted a 30" COOL WAY attic fan ($99.98) that was a breeze on a hot, summer day. 8' X 14' patio covers ($137 up) were looking up. Lumber prices were advertised as the lowest around, and we tended to agree that Sutherland would M.A.S.H. most of the competition. Check directory for other locations. MC, V

U should Plumb-It to this do-it-yourself shop and save. They sell pipes, hot water heaters, tools, potties and much more. Everything you need to unclog your problem. So plunge in. Personnel were very helpful in explaining how to fix your particular problem. CK, MC, SC, V

***
U-PLUMB IT PLUMBING SUPPLY
1612 Gessner
Houston
Tel. 932-8151
Sun-S 9-9

BUYING SERVICES

The Houston Consumer Center is a sister organization of the phenomenally successful Dallas buying service. The Houston Consumer Center can get you the rock bottom price on everything from autos to appliances and watches to wallpaper. They can save you loads on carpets, drapes, stereos, TV's, jewelry, typewriters, tires and much more. Brands such as RCA, ZENITH, TOSHIBA, SONY, MAYTAG, LITTON, AMANA, BASSETT, PANASONIC and MOULINEX are typical. Membership in the Houston Consumer Center is a bargain. Annual corporate rate is $7.50, 3-year corporate rate is $15. Annual individual rate is $9, 3-year individual rate is $18. (Beware of any buying service which charges over $50 to join. Too often, they sign up 1,000 members and then move to Brazil.) CK, MC, V

****
HOUSTON CONSUMER CENTER
5325 Glenmont
Houston
Tel. 666-5507
M-F 10-6/S 9-2

CAMERA AND FILM

Smile! Say, "cheap!" It was a snap to save money at Floyd's, a prints of a place. Twelve or twenty prints of 110 film were $1.50 plus .31/print, less 20%. For twenty prints, that's .31 each. Enlargements for 110 film: 5 X 7 ($2) and 8 X 12 ($4.10); 135 film: 5 X 7 ($1.50) and 8 X 12 ($3.50). CK

**
FLOYDS FOTO INC.
835 Studewood
Houston
Tel. 862-1670
M-F 8-5:30

CARPETS

***
**ASSOCIATED
CARPET
BROKERS, INC.**
1414 Blalock Road
Houston
Tel. 465-7352
M-S 9-6

My kid is a broker. Last Sunday, at Grandma's, he broker dish, he broker lamp and he broker record for most damage done by a grandchild. Associated Brokers fared better. We saw 50% discounts on first quality, samples and overruns by KELLER, HORIZON, FLINT CREST and more. Their shaggy, low overhead type warehouse saved us money in carpeting our own pad. We saw KELLER Elegance at $13.99/yd. compared with $24.99 at a major department store. Most was $5.99/yd. to $13.99/yd. Cut a pile of money from your carpet expense here. Check directory for other locations. CK, MC, V

**
CARPET RACK
109 E. Little York
Houston
Tel. 691-3728
M-S 9-6

Carpet Racked up 20-30% savings. The most expensive carpet we saw was $17.95/yd., installed. Top brands, too, like ARMSTRONG, PEPPERELL and ALDON. Indoor, outdoor was $11.95 installed (reg. $14.95), and vinyl flooring was $10.95 to $16.95 installed. CK

COD INSTALLERS
9577 Country Creek
Houston
Tel. 995-6862
M-F 10-8:30/S 8-6

COD is interested only in the installation of carpet. They charge $5/yd., plus pad. They also can get carpet at wholesale if they are permitted to do the installation. For example, KELLER-BRAVO, builders grade would cost $3.40/yd. plus $5/yd. installation. Lifetime guarantee on workmanship, manufacturer's guarantee on carpet. Makes cents to us to go COD. CK, MC

****
**HOUSTON
CONSUMER CENTER**

See write up under "Buying Services."

CHEAP THRILLS

**ASTRO CITY
AMUSEMENTS**
Spring-Cypress Road
Houston
Tel. 370-1844
      376-5702
Call for hours

Astro no questions and I'll tell you no lies. Astro City Amusements is FUN! Good money-maker for promotions and carnivals. Your organization picks the ticket price and takes 30%. Three kiddie rides are provided (insurance included)—a 30' X 30' moon walk, a cute lady bug ride and a mechanical horse that pulls a cart. Plan ahead! Very popular amusement, and we're not kid-ding. $

This free tour was a self-conducted, educational hop through a fully automated brewery. They also had an aviary behind the brewery, filled with exotic birds. Barley had enough energy left to partake in the free samples at the end. We were Busch-ed. FREE

BUSCH BREWERY
9-10 E. at Geilhorn Exit
Houston
Tel. 675-2311
M-S 10-5
Sun & Holidays 12-6

Before you go down for the third time, take the plunge and join up for free Red Cross swimming classes. If you're not a swimmer, then call the listed number and receive a free listing of all the locations for tennis, golf, bike and hiking trails. FREE

CITY OF HOUSTON PARKS AND RECREATION
2999 South Wayside
Houston
Tel. 641-4111
Call for hours

Watch it! You might catch string fever after becoming a member of this society. For a $10/yr. membership, you'll be eligible for a minimum of four concerts by well-known artists, a minimum of two recitals, weekly discussions, info on concerts, workshops, scholarships and a monthly newsletter to keep you abreast of strings. This is a non-profit organization, with about 200 members. $

CLASSICAL GUITAR SOCIETY
1401 Richmond
Houston
Tel. 528-5666
Call for hours

Things do go better with Coke, particularly when the drinks are free. A peppy, free educational tour, Dr. We observed the real thing: the complete bottling process, a display of Coke bottles throughout the years and an entertaining movie that added life to the tour. Free cokes during the movie as well as a free pencil and pad souvenir. Must call ahead for reservations for group tours. FREE

COCA-COLA BOTTLING CO.
2800 Bissonnet
Houston
Tel. 664-3451
M-F 10-1:30

Is your participle dangling (so badly that it shows)? Well, let the University of Houston assistance service help you tuck it in. Their objective is to give free grammar information (via the telephone) to all of you math majors. FREE

GRAMMAR HOT LINE
Houston
Tel. 749-3074
M-F 9-4

HOUSTON PUBLIC LIBRARY
500 McKinney Ave.
Houston
Tel. 224-5441
M-S 10-6

A cheap lot (of films). We checked out a Lon Chaney movie from the over 2000 films available free to the public. Everything from silent movies up to the TV hit "Roots". Even checked out a 16 mm projector too, but advance notice was required to secure one. Sure beat the opera. I could Beverly sit Sills with all the suspense happening in my living room. It was reel-ly exciting. FREE

THEATER UNDER THE STARS
1999 West Gray
Miller Theater
Houston
Tel. 522-9701
M-F 9-6

In order to present a successful play you need three things—the play, the actors and an audience, and each must contribute something. Act-cept for performances at the Miller Theater. They are free! Plays are funded by the city, foundations, businesses and individual donations. Join the thousands who attend "TUTS" every year and have a good tomb. FREE

Films are periodically shown at University Center (U of H), Museum of Fine Arts and Rice University for $1.50 or less. Some are really movie-ing experiences. Call for dates and times.

Museum of Fine Arts
1001 Bissonnet
Brown Auditorium
Houston
Tel. 526-1361

Rice University
Media Center
Ent. No. 7 off University Blvd.
Houston
Tel. 527-4853 (tape)

University of Houston
University Center
Program Counsel
Houston
Tel. 749-1435
    749-3456 (tape)

CLEANERS AND LAUNDRIES

**
RIDDLES COIN WASHATERIA
2028 East TC Jester
Houston
Tel. 862-0202
M-F 7-7/S 7-6

Riddle: Do-it-yourself dry cleaning saves (   ). Coin-cidentally, its money. A mens' 3-pc. suit was $3.25 (reg. $4.75) and a mens' 2-pc. suit was $2.90 (reg. $3.75). A ladies' 3-pc. suit was $3.50 (reg. $4.85) and ladies' slacks were $1.60/ea. (reg. $2.60). 25-35% discounts across the (ironing) board. A complete washeteria was on premises, too. $

CONSUMER SERVICES
Good Help Is Not Hard To Find

COUNTY AGENCIES

Many states have consumer help on the local level. Most counties have at least one agency to assist you, and will, if possible, forward your problem to the office nearest you. Houston offers help through this agency:

Assistant District Attorney
Consumer Fraud Division
301 San Jacinto
Houston, Texas 77002
(713) 228-8311, ext. 7493

STATE AGENCIES

State agencies are taking a more active role in conflicts between consumers and merchants. Approximately 10,000 complaints are handled per year in Texas with 75% of cases resolved successfully! Agencies are run by your tax dollar for you, but only deal with in-state problems. Allow four weeks for complaint(s) to be processed.

Assistant Attorney General
369 One Main Plaza
Houston, Texas 77002
(713) 228-0701

FEDERAL AGENCIES

The Feds are getting better at solving the problems of consumer complaints. Congressmen and senators are ultra-sensitive to unsettled complaints via federal agencies. There are numerous agencies consumers can approach, but the most convenient is the Federal Information Center. Call and define your problem and they'll lead you to the correct agency—USDA, CAB, EPA, etc. Good for out of state problems.

Federal Information Center
Houston (713) 226-5711

CONSUMER SERVICES

BETTER BUSINESS BUREAU

The BBB should be one of the first contacted. They know pertinent facts about companies and how to approach a complaint for the best results. Although they have no legal jurisdiction, they offer third party arbitration that can bring decision out of court.

BBB of Metropolitan Houston, Inc.
1212 Main St., Suite 533
Houston, Texas 77002
(713) 224-6111

MANUFACTURERS

Companies can seldom make money selling you something only once. Valid complaints always interest businesses so product defects can be remedied. The best procedure is to write the president of the parent company using his personal name. Some basic research required, but results can be achieved. Believe us, they care what the public thinks!

MEDIA AND ACTION LINES

Most newspapers, magazines, radio and TV stations welcome complaints about their advertisers. No one wants "bad press". The Houston Chronicle is especially interested. If you dial W-A-T-C-H-E-M, you'll get a recorded message which will take your phone number and info about your complaint. Nothing is guaranteed—but it's worth a try!

Houston Chronicle
801 Texas Avenue
Houston, Texas 77002
(713) 928-2436

SMALL CLAIMS COURT

Have your day in court with or without an attorney, for a minimal filing charge. If you have a worthwhile complaint on any amount up to $500, the small claims court is the place to go. In Texas, the Justice of the Peace handles small claims, with appeals going to the county courts. This court uses ordinary language and low court and legal costs. May request jury trial with 24 hour notice. Check the location of the nearest JP court for filing.

TRADE ASSOCIATIONS

Call the BBB or Chamber of Commerce to find local industry groups. Organizations like the Carpet and Rug Institute or the Jewelers Vigilance Committee make sure their trade's businesses are fair and live up to the standards of the industry. A good source for action.

CRAFTY STUFF

You don't have to be a Barn yesterday to appreciate this picture frame store. We found custom-made wood, metal and leather frames. Good prices—we spotted a 24" X 36" wood frame for $28.50. Big selection. Located in an attractive yellow barn. $

**
ART BARN
GALLERY
500 N. Post Oak Rd.
Houston
Tel. 681-7744
T-F 10-5/S 10-1

How great is thou art? Well, you won't want to brush off some of the bargains we saw at this craft and hobby shop. Easel-ly 15% lower on items like frames, yarn, paint, tools and brushes. They have a big following among the local artists, and have framed many of them. CK, MC, SC, V

**
SUN BELT ART
SUPPLY, INC.
2056 Wirt
Houston
Tel. 683-9703
M-F 8:30-6/S 9-3

Get the picture, then frame it yourself. Prices were $3.25/ft. for metal frames and $4/ft. for gold wood, less 45%. Glass was extra. Personnel were helpful in selection and framing. CK

***
WAREHOUSE
PICTURE
FRAMING
11450 Bissonnet
Houston
Tel. 933-6599
T-Th 10-6/F-S 10-4

DENTAL

We're not pulling your leg when we say you can walk in here and have your teeth pulled for free. They only charge for material used—silver for fillings or gold for crowns, etc. Work is provided by juniors and seniors. Ad leasd we feld bedder do know the sdudend we used godd an "F" on his repord card. FREE

*UNIVERSITY OF
TEXAS DENTAL
BRANCH
Texas Medical Center
Houston
Tel. 792-4056 (adults)
      792-4141 (children age 12 and under)
M-F 9-11*

DEPARTMENT STORES

****
MARSHALL'S
7055 S.W. Freeway
(next to Target)
Houston
Tel. 988-3200
M-S 9:30-9:30

The big secret is that they buy AFTER the season has started. 20-60% off on first quality goods (a few irregulars). POLO, GLORIA VANDERBILT, PIERRE CARDIN, VAN HEUSEN, MANHATTAN, BRITTANIA, GEOFFREY BEENE, ARROW and CHRISTIAN DIOR. We saw MANHATTAN shirts for $8.99 up, velour shirts for $12.99 up and BRITTANIA jeans for $16.99. Decorator throw pillows were $3.99 up. And we judged the kid's clothing completely innocent of high prices. Thur good, Marshall. Also, 9401 Katy Freeway, 465-8211. CK

EYEWEAR

NV
CONTAX DUPLICATION SERVICE
P.O. Box 29333
San Antonio, TX 78229

My kid got rid of his bifocals because he decided smooching was a contact sport. If you agree with him here's a place to get them cheap. We found that Contax offered single vision hard lenses ($24.99/ea.) and soft lenses ($47.99/ea.). Why not order extra pairs in different colors? Write for prices for hard or soft lenses. Satisfaction guaranteed, or your old eye problem back. $

****
ROYAL OPTICAL

See under Old Listings, EYEWEAR.

FURNITURE: CUSTOM

NR
HIS ACRYLIC COMPANY
1035 Gessner, No. E
Houston
Tel. 468-6787
Call for hours

And His public came to the spot of His workshop wanting gifts of myrrh, frankincense and acrylic. But only the latter they found. We discovered that Paul Panto designed tables, chairs, bar stools, shelves and various other unique forms of furniture. He struck us as being an honest man doing an honest days work for an honest wage. He was hard to find. Behind the Skelly tire store in a warehouse area. CK

They tell us "B & W" will soon change its name to "The Furniture Idea." The ideas we saw were good ones. We spotted 20-35% savings on upholstered furniture and about 10% off on mattresses. We noted brands such as BASSETT, THERAPEDIC and NASCO. Selection was good and the store looked like Mama had just cleaned. CK, AE, MC, V

***
**B & W FURNITURE
WAREHOUSE**
10175 Harwin
Houston
Tel. 981-8638
M-Th 10-8/F-S 10-6
Sun Browsing 12-5

Three chairs for Bright Ideas. We found tables and chairs by CONANT BALL. Hoop arm chairs were $105, hoop side chairs were $99.50 and a 38" X 68" dining table with two 12" leaves was $426. A butcher block style chair by OTTO GER-DAU (natural finish and woven seat) was $61.50. Store was filled with old fashion wood furniture. Found old time bobbins too, for $3-$20. CK, MC, V

**
**BRIGHT IDEAS
FURNITURE**
3202 Fondren
Houston
Tel. 977-1560
M-T, Th-F 10-8
W, S 10-6

Lattice pay. There's a company in Houston doing wood lattice work for a variety of indoor, outdoor uses. Everything from doors, etageres, window coverings, patio coverings, decorative trim for the house, screens, tables and frames are made by using these lattice panels. Panels are made from redwood, cedar or pine. Our panel voted them a unique service. CK, DC, MC, V

**NR
CUSTOM LATTICE**
2505 S. Shephard
Houston
Tel. 528-5152
M-F 9-5/S 10-6

Curses! Some things should happen more often than once a month. We learned they have a sale the first Saturday of every month. We found pictures, mirrors, lamps, antiques and upholstered furniture at 20-50% savings during these periodic sales. We saw a green velvet wingback chair for $215 (reg. $355) and a love seat for $480 (reg. $800). Personnel helped ease the discomforts of shopping. CK, MC, V

**NR
THE DESIGN STUDIO**
2431 Rice Blvd.
Houston
Tel. 529-4137
M-S 9-5

**
**DESIGNER
FURNITURE
WAREHOUSE**
3750 West Chase Dr.
Houston
Tel. 780-0221
M-F 10-8/S 9-7

If you like yours king size and firm and at a 35-40% discount, you'll love their beds. We saw 25-40% discounts on first quality chairs, dinettes and a sofa, Tucker. They say they'll beat anyone else's prices. Could be. CK, MC, V

**NR
FINGERS
FURNITURE**
4001 Gulf Freeway
Houston
Tel. 221-4441
Periodic Sale 10-9

Be here early for this once-a-year clearance sale. People wait in line outside for hours to be the first to get their Fingers on the sale merchandise. Savings up to 50% on furniture and accessories. Call for info on exact dates. CK

**NO STAR
THE FURNITURE
FARM**
2323 Wirt Road
Houston
No phone listed
M-S 9-9

A trip to the funny farm would probably have been nicer than our visit to The Furniture Farm. We should have guessed it was going to be crazy when we drove up to the cluster of pink buildings. Inside we found three dirty rooms with uneven floors loaded with furniture. They advertised "new furniture at cheap prices." We felt they had transposed "cheap" and "new." CK, MC, V

****
**HOUSTON
CONSUMER CENTER**

See write up under "Buying Services."

***
THE INSIDE STORY
767 Kenrick
Houston
Tel. 820-3030
M-T, Th-F 10-8/S 10-6
Sun Browsing 12-5

The Inside Story is big bargains on designer furniture. We found entire pit groups for $695 and sofa-loveseat combinations for $389. Sofa-sogood? We don't want to table the conversation, but we found an octagonal pecan, cane under glass with brass accents, MIKADO table for $245. Most of the pieces came in over 300 fabric selections. Everything from designer prints to Haitian cottons. And that's the story. Other locations: Dallas, Richardson, Oklahoma City, Tulsa. CK, MC, V

**NR
JOSKES**
6666 Makawa
Houston
Tel. 644-2661
Periodic Sale 10-6

Save up to 50% on Joske's three times a year furniture clearance sale. Call the store for dates. It's a biggie and merchandise is all first quality, of course. CK

Rise and shine! Check out Suniland's once a year (at least) warehouse sale. We saw living room furniture reduced 50-75%, SEALY bedding at half price, bookcase wall units at $99.50, a large selection of fabric remnants reduced 50-90% and carpet roll-ends at 40-60% off. Call for dates on the next sale. All sales final. Extra charge for delivery. $

NR
SUNILAND WAREHOUSE
4001 Briarpark
Houston
Tel. 780-9885
Periodic Sale 10-6

You can get heaps of cheaps here. It was hard for us to determine the quality of their goods, but it didn't look half bad. We found a 3-pc. living room set for $195. Included were a sofa, love seat and chair, all in herculon. Also saw a twin bedroom set for $80. CK, MC, V

*
TEXAS WHOLESALE FURNITURE
15033 South Main
Houston
Tel. 721-7394
Sun-S 10-7

Warehouse stored all kinds of furnishings—first quality, closeouts, discontinued lines and some damaged freight. Lots of it was gathered from large area department stores. Found 33-50% savings on everything from barstools to living room suites. Saw a king-size sleeper sofa for $289 (reg. $449), oak bedroom suites at $498 (reg. $698), sofa and love seat combos for $359 (reg. $595) and beautiful glass and walnut coffee tables at $129 (reg. $199). Labels abound like BASSETT, TRENDSETTER and BROYHILL. No air conditioning in the warehouse. CK, MC, V

***
WAREHOUSE FURNITURE
1810 Franklin
Houston
Tel. 228-2022
M-S 10-6

Wells was deep in better name-brand furniture at 25-50% savings. Strike it rich with BURLINGTON HOUSE, WESTWOOD, STANLEY, PETERS-RIVINGTON and COLEMAN. First quality sofa-sleepers ($445 up), lamps ($50), roll top desks ($525 up) and framed DALHART WINDBERG prints ($50-$150) were not much more than a drip in the bucket when compared to regular retail. Located in an old 2-story house. Free delivery with any $200 purchase. CK

****
WELLS FURNITURE
4500 Caroline
Houston
Tel. 523-8872
M-S 10-6/S 1-5

FURNITURE: OFFICE

**

**DISCOUNT OFFICE
FURNITURE**
5714 Clarewood
Houston
Tel. 666-8767
M-F 9-5:30/S 9-2

Make your secretary a Princess. She'll feel
like she's wearing a crown with the trio we
saw: a 30" X 48" walnut desk ($179),
a posture back secretary chair ($70) and a 4
drawer file cabinet for $115 (reg. $325).
File this one in your memory. CK, MC, V

****

**HOUSTON
CONSUMER CENTER**

See write-up under "Buying Services."

FURNITURE: UNASSEMBLED

***

FURNITURE TO GO
3400 Fondren
Houston
Tel. 780-8063
T-W, F-S 10-6
M, Th 10-9

We saw loads of unassembled contemporary
furniture, such as walnut microwave oven
stands for $49.95 (reg. $69), oak and glass
sewing carts for $49 (reg. $69.95), knee-
hole desks for $89 (reg. $129) and brewers
chairs for $36 (reg. $58). Take furniture
home and assemble yourself. CK, SC, V

FURNITURE: USED

*

FLASHBACK
2502 Ralph
Houston
Tel. 526-0616
T-S 10-5:30

If you are over 50, you'll fall over when you
see their prices. If you are under 50, you'll
think its a good deal. Take your pick from
the 30's, 40's or 50's in furnishings and
accessories piled up in this old house in
Montrose. We saw a 1930 curio cabinet
($450), a buffet ($250) and 1940 simplicity
patterns ($1/ea.). We flashed by displays of
bow ties, shoes, costume jewelry, hats and
gloves. Manager David Scarbrough had the
place looking like a museum. CK

**

J'S TRADING POST
9753 Long Point
Houston
Tel. 467-1115
M-F 10-8/S 10-5

J's—Not Just Junk. We found cameras,
crutches, musical instruments and even old
cash registers. Some marked, some not. We
did get a fix on KENMORE sewing machines from $90-$140. They will "deal"
on price. CK

Let's face it. Chartreuse is NOT the in color anymore. Tote that funny colored sofa to On Consignment. This resale shop will accept your well-conditioned furniture and act as your sales agent. Only quality merchandise is accepted. Unfortunely, prices were well above where we had hoped to find them. They had lamps, mirrors, pictures and lotsa furniture. CK, MC, V

*
ON CONSIGNMENT
11146 Westheimer
Houston
Tel. 783-3637
M-S 10-6

GENEALOGY

Before we suggest having your family tree traced in Texas (by way of the 1850 census), we'd like to remind you that heredity is what causes the parents of teen-agers to wonder about each other! Nevertheless, if you wish your family history retraced, the cost is only $5. $

NV
HAVEN WELLS
2801 Patricia
La Marque, TX 77568

GIFTS

This is truly a place to find a unique gift. We discovered old newspapers, engravings, magazines, books and pictures. There were a number of completely intact magazines from the early 1900's. Shop was small, well-organized and prices were reasonable (starting at $3). CK, MC, V

***
A PAGE OUT OF HISTORY COLLECTIBLES
11450 Bissonnet
No. 301
Houston
Tel. 933-6170
M-S 9-4

A bum asked me for $500 for plane fare to England. He said he had a job as an 'obo with the Royal Philharmonic. Now, THAT is a Creative Touch. The two ladies that run this shop have a special touch for creating beautifully crafted gift items. We admired their stained glass, macrame and paintings. Prices were moderate, starting at $1. They offered classes in handicrafts. Call for subjects, dates, times and prices. CK

**
CREATIVE TOUCH GIFTS & CRAFTS
11450 Bissonnet
No. 303
Houston
Tel. 933-6750
T-S 9:30-5

***
ENAMEL EMPORIUM
113 Meyerland Plaza
Houston
•Tel. 667-6999
M-W, F 9-5:30/Th 9-8
S 10-6

Cloissone cat can scratch you. Cloisonne vases can excite you. Learn to make your own or buy those made right here in Houston by Oriental craftsmen at The Enamel Emporium. We found the workmanship to be superior. The prices on their vases, boxes, plates, jewelry, bowls and bottles were from $3 up. Ask about their enameling classes ($65). The process Confucius until we took the course. CK, MC, V

NV
SADDLE BLANKET CO.
Box 12360
El Paso, Texas 79912

I knew an insurance agent who wanted me to get blanket coverage on my bed. I told him I'd sleep on it. I got a better deal from El Paso saddle blanket company. Genuine hand-woven Mexican sarapes with beautiful, bright colors. Six sizes from .95 to $13.50. Write for free catalog. CK

*
TWO SIDES
331 Meyerland Plaza
Houston
Tel. 667-4533
Call for hours

They advertised unusual gifts at "very good prices." Often, one man's "good price" is another man's "too much." They do stock unusual gifts, such as hand-painted tiles, stainless steel skewers, copperware, escargot pans, terra cotta flower pots and hand sewn items. Too much. Exchanges only. CK, MC, V

GLASS REPAIR

**THE GLASS DOCTOR
TRANS EUROPA
ANTIQUES**
2528 Amherst
Houston
Tel. 524-5002
T-S 10-5

Having trouble seeing with your glass eye? If it's chipped, broken or cracked, this doctor will fix it. With crystal costs rising, we thought these prices were reasonable. Repairs on wine glasses ($8-$10), pitcher with chipped spout ($15) and large decanters ($25-$30) seemed to be in the right range. Repairs also on china, ceramics and porcelain. CK

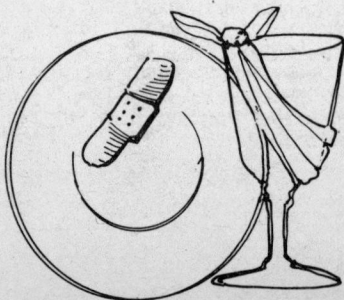

GRAPHIC DESIGN

A Kinko Graphic is NOT the centerfold in the Swine Breeder's Journal. It's a great place for cheap printing and copying. The shop had a catchall bulletin board filled with strange and unique ads, petitions, pictures and cards. Copying was done for as little as .03½/page. Cheap sheets! In addition to regular copying, they did film processing, passport photos, binding, printing and color copies. Other location at 2811 Main St. CK, V

****
KINKO'S GRAPHIC
2368 Rice Blvd.
Houston
Tel. 667-9817
M-Th 8:30-7/F 8:30-6
S 9-5/Sun 11-4

They work on projects from simple invitations to the most complicated architectural drafting. Do single customer jobs or advanced industrial work. Have five years experience creating an image through design. Calligraphy, posters, mailers, announcements and invitations. Fee is either hourly or flat fee depending on the job. CK

LINEAGRAPH CORP.
3518 Travis, Suite 110
Houston
Tel. 527-0147
M-F 8-5

GROCERIES

Because food prices fluctuate so widely, day to day, we have not rated the food outlets. We believe we have given you enough information, though, to find good, wholesome vegies at down to earth prices.

Let Charles Chip away at your appetite, without shattering your budget. He home delivers excellent potato chips, pretzels and cookies. A one pound can of potato chips was $2 plus .80 deposit and a three pound can was $5.40 (plus $2.65 deposit on the can). Usually has an excellent assortment of cookies for Christmas, with the quality being "a la Neiman's" and the cost approximating "a uh NABISCO." $

CHARLIE'S CHIPS
6325 Beverly Hill
Houston
Tel. 781-3278
M-F 8-5

Parton us, but we discovered that this Dolly has nice buns (and a twinkie in her eye). Save 30-50% on day old products returned by the delivery trucks. Products often as fresh as a grocery store. CK

DOLLY MADISON
2030 Wirt
Houston
Tel. 688-4666
M-S 9-7/Sun 12-6

EILENBERGER'S BAKERY
P.O. Box 710
Palestine, TX 75801
Tel. (214) 729-2176

Hey, fruitcake! If you can't cake it with you, then have it shipped. This mail-order bakery dates back to 1898, and expects to ship out close to four million pounds of fruitcake this season. Select from various sizes and prices: $7.15/2 lb., $9.65/3 lb. and $14.95/5 lb. Cakes usually shipped same day as ordered. Also have pecan cakes. CK

FRED REYES PRODUCE & INDOOR-OUTDOOR PLANTS
Bissonnet between
Beechnut & Fondren
Houston
No phone listed
Sun-S 8-8

Farmers Reyes produce and Reyes sells it. We found Fred Reyes' open air stand on Bissonnet. He had loads of peaches, cantaloupe, watermelon, green beans and tomatoes (enriched by the Reyes of the sun) at prices well below grocery stores. They receive fresh produce daily. Lots of indoor-outdoor plants, too. CK

FROBERG'S FARM
Old Manvel Road
Alvin
Tel. 585-3531
Call for hours

This farm beets the competition, hands down. To get there, truck on down Hwy. 35 to Alvin, turnip Hwy. 6, then take a left at the blinking light. There you'll find broccoli every kind of fruit and vegetable imaginable. Buy by the bushel or pound. They lettuce pick peaches, blackberries, eggplant, etc., ourselves to save more money. Prices were about 30% off grocery store. CK

GINO'S ITALIAN BAKERY
6515 Bissonnet
Houston
Tel. 776-0744
M-Th 8-8/F-S 8-9

Gino who makes the best Italian pastries? Gino drove us nuts with his super delicious, genuine Italian pastries, like cannoli, pasticciotti, Italian breads, plus wedding and birthday cakes. Wedding cakes were $3.99 up and rum birthday cakes won our respect for $6.99/ea. Cookies were $1.20-$1.80/doz. Italian bread was .60 a loaf. Try their original Italian pizza, too. CK

GOW BEE HONEY FARM
5305 Highway Blvd.
Katy
Tel. 371-2858
     529-8736
M-F 8-4

Hive never seen so much honey. We combed the grounds and inspected over 5000 hives (more than you'd find at an allergist's convention). The Gows own a plant to process their honey. They turn out products such as honey-herb salad dressing, marinade, honey orange peel spread, honey facial scrub and honey-mustard sauce. They also sell a great line of smoked meats (won't hurt your lungs). Drive out and save 15%. The educational portion is free. CK

We saved about 20% on dead cow flesh. We liked the brisket at $1.59/lb. (reg. $1.89), pork ribs at $1.59/lb., whole fryers at $1.79/lb. and best cut pork chops for $1.79/lb. Atmosphere was what you would expect in an old fashioned meat shop, complete with glass front cases. Usually have weekly specials. Friendly service. CK, MC, V

MIDWEST BEEF CO. RETAIL MARKET
1201 N. Post Oak
Houston
Tel. 686-4386
T-F 9-6/S 9-5

Have no re-Morse about buying everything from pencil sharpeners to pepperoni sausage at wholesale prices. We discovered they sold candies, gums and school supplies, in bulk only, out of their warehouse. We got Morse for our money by buying ALMOND JOY ($4.50/case), CAREFREE gum ($3.60/case), HERSHEY kisses ($4.50/120), pepperoni sausage ($4/30) and NESTLE'S Crunch ($6.75/120). $

MORSE WHOLESALE
3302 Canal
Houston
Tel. 223-8361
Call for hours

Here's a "Y" where anyone can get in. They carried nine varieties of cakes and 21 different kinds of pies. Everything has been made from scratch by the same cooks for 18 years. We topped off our visit with a three layer 8" carrot cake for $7. Pies were $3.75/ea. Allow 24 hours for orders to be filled. $

ORIGINAL Y-W CAFETERIA BAKERY
1521 Texas
Houston
Tel. 236-0030
M-F 7-8

Shopping at Orowheat's budget outlet is not a half-baked idea. With grocery costs climbing everyday, why not save some dough by shopping this day-old store? We found little difference between the quality of the bread here and at the supermarket. We saved 25-50%. And that's the crust of the batter. No bun intended. CK

OROWHEAT BAKERY CO. BUDGET STORE
2033-A Bingle Rd.
Houston
Tel. 932-6273
M-S 10-6

20-50% off on baked goods. Some day old, some over-under weight. Best time to go is in the morning. $

PEPPERIDGE FARMS THRIFT SHOP
1020 FM 1960
Houston
Tel. 440-7916
M-S 10-6

Shrimp and crab delivered at reasonable prices. Call Kathy Holtzman. $

SHRIMP
Tel. 765-5653

We were looking for a teeny little guy. What we found was Bill Murray, a regular person. He said he would deliver shrimp to any home or office. It comes packed in ice, enclosed in styrofoam containers. CK

SHRIMPMAN
Houston
Tel. 339-2159

39

**THE THIRD DAY
HERBAL HOME &
GARDENS**
9406 Alberne
Houston
Tel. 776-2215
T-F 10-2/S 10-5

If you haven't discovered the joy of cooking with herbs and spices, you are really missing the second best thing in life. The Third Day stocked over 100 varieties of herbs and herbal related products. It is a true "living herbs" nursery. We found that Marilyn Woods, the owneress, gives lectures to garden clubs. She carries only herbs that grow well in Houston. The first best thing in life? Why, it's eating all that wonderful cooking, of course. What in the world did you think it was? CK, MC, V

**WONDER HOSTESS
BAKERY THRIFT
SHOP**
8612 Long Point
Houston
No phone listed
M-S 9-7

As Harry Belafonte might say, "Da-a-y-y old, Da-a-a-y-y old!" A little age on the goodies doesn't hurt. Honey buns ($1/box), fried pies ($1/9), hamburgers and hot dog buns ($1.09/3 bags) and bread (.25/loaf) knead no bargain explanation. Roll in Wednesday for super bargain day. CK

HAIR CARE

*BALDWIN BEAUTY
SCHOOL*
8327 Long Point
Houston
Tel. 464-1659
T-S 8:30-5

At these prices, even the Bald-win. Long Point is the permanent address. For $12.50 you may have one, too. Other points we'd like to brush up on were the shampoo and set $4.25, haircut $4, tint $6, facials $10 and sculptured nails $17. On Tuesday and Wednesday they offer senior citizen haircuts for $2.50. $

*BELLAIRE BEAUTY
COLLEGE*
5014 Bellaire Blvd.
Houston
Tel. 666-2318
T-S 8-3:30

What the heck. Van Gogh didn't look too bad with just one ear. Haircuts by students were $5. We got a shampoo and set for only $3.50. A shampoo while standing was the same price. Mrs. Stevens (supervisor) made sure everything was even. Perms were $15 and sculptured nails were $10. The service was very good. $

*BOB WEBB'S BARBER
SHOP*
1832 Wirt
Houston
Tel. 682-9176
T-F 8-5/S 8-3

No need to tuffet out, Ms. Muffet. Bob Webb will trim those tresses for $5. He cuts with care and expertise. Weave never seen anything like it. Everything from burrs to long hair styles for men and women. CK

Not by the hair of your chinny, chin, chin. Beards trimmed for $4. Regular men's haircuts $1.50 or styled $5-$6. Gave .75 discount to senior citizens, firemen, policemen and members of the military. Good first aid kit. $

D'LYNN L. BARBER COLLEGE
9821 Katy Fwy.
Houston
Tel. 461-3800
M-F 8-7/S 8-5

A fraudulent bruin is obviously a shampooh. Nothing phony about the terrific shampoo and set we got here for $3.60. If you can bear it, facials (by appt. only) were really uplifting at $5 up. Haircuts were but a grizzly $5. We discovered perms were $15, tints were $7.50, bleach was $13.50 (hello, Dolly) and frosting was $12.50. $

GARDEN OAKS BEAUTY COLLEGE
3830 N. Shepherd
Houston
Tel. 694-0065
      695-6803
T-Th 9:30-7/F 9:30-3
S 8-2

The students at Rice Academy were real class cutters. That should please their customers, however. Men's and women's haircuts were $4. Perms were $18-$24, frostings $18.50, sculptured nails $18.50 and eyelashes $9. We gave the students at this Academy B plus for skills and pricing. $

RICE ACADEMY BEAUTY SCHOOL
8701 Long Point
Houston
Tel. 468-7979
T-Th 9-7/F 8-3/S 8-12

The Wittee Road scholars are learning to be clever beauticians. We spotted prices that were no joke. Shampoo/set was $3.50, haircuts $5 and perms $17.50 up. Wigs washed and styled for $10. $

SPRING BRANCH BEAUTY COLLEGE
1206 Wittee Road
Houston
Tel. 464-5647
T-F 9:30-3/S 8-2

HANDBAGS

Bag-nificent is the word for these women's handbags and accessories. Excellent discounts of 20-50% on clutches $10.90, canvas totes $5, PIERRE CARDIN bags $43.90, scarves $1 and earrings $2.50-$3. Ear piercing was $5.90. Also saw LAND bags $59.90-$63.90. Other designer merchandise included CHRISTIAN DIOR. Displays were neat and nicely arranged with prices marked. One of the best places in the world (Houston, anyway) to buy a bag, Dad. MC, SC, V

****
BAG WORLD
7144 Southwest Frwy.
Houston
Tel. 981-6844
T-W, F-S 10-6
M, Th 10-8

*
**BEST HEALTH
FOODS**
4326 Washington
Houston
Tel. 869-4784
M-S 9:30-6

This wasn't the Best Health Foods store we've visited. Relatively small stock, but they did have a complete selection of RICHLIFE and DITTO vitamins. Vitamins are rarely discounted unless they're old and actually should not "B" sold in that condition. You "C," they loose their potency after "A" certain time. And that's "D" truth. CK

***
HEAVENLY BODY
2549 Gessner
Houston
Tel. 462-9934
M-F 9-8/S 10-4

No wings, no harps, no kidding. Heavenly Body is a fitness center, dedicated to the health and well being of womankind in general and the owners of the business specifically. Ladies (only) may sign up for the whole works—diets, weight trimming, machines, exercise instruction, sauna and showers, for the very reasonable price of $49 for four months. The first visit was free. This is one of the best deals we have found. CK

**
**A WHOLE FOOD
STORE**
2437 University
Houston
Tel. 523-4263
M-S 10-7

This was only parsley A Whole Food Store. It was principally a specialty shop featuring a large selection of herbs and spices. Which is what it was mint to be. Herbs sprouted from .29 to $1.79 (half ounce minimum). We spent a lot of thyme ginger-ly browsing. They had some dill-y displays. Also saw accessories, such as tea strainers .99, perfumes $1.95 and a spine roller $19.95. Nice as a rose, Mary. CK

****
**YE SEEKERS
HORIZON**
9336 Westview
Houston
Tel. 461-0857
M-S 10-9

If ye believe ye have good health, then ye've got everything. Check out Ye Seekers Horizon, anyway. Ye will discover one of the largest health stores in the country. Ye'll find vitamins, cosmetics, minerals, proteins, organic meats and vegetables and at yeast a hundred other items. They also had an extensive metaphysical book selection for ye mind and a restaurant next door for ye body. From ghost to toast. MC

HOME REPAIRS

Bandy is dandy. He was recommended to us by a lady doctor who said he was super honest and reasonable. Service charges varied, depending on distance traveled. We were told he quoted prices over the phone. He has a lot of fans. That's cool. CK

BANDY AIR AND HEATING
9941 Rowlett
Houston
Tel. 946-1544
M-F 9-5

HOUSE SITTERS

Rock-a-bye, mansion, your boss has left town. We found that this service provides your home sweet home with daily attention while you're on vacation or a weekend excursion. For $6/day they'll turn your lights on and off, pick up your newspapers, feed your pets and pick up your mail. Staff is fully insured. CK

NR
AVAILABLE SERVICES CORP.
Houston
Tel. 524-5759
Call for hours

JEWELRY

They wouldn't get top billing for their performance when we visited. Their summer stock seemed skimpy and discounts weren't crystal clear. We found 14K class rings from $85-$110. $125 for special designs. Diamonds were marked down 20%. Not bad, if the regular price was reasonable. CK, MC, V

*
BILLINGS JEWELERS
10020 Long Point
Houston
Tel. 468-8646
M-W, F 9-6/Th 9:30-8
S 9-5:30

See write-up under "Buying Services."

****
HOUSTON CONSUMER CENTER

Can only describe Klein's as a lamb shop, complete with shepherd and flock. The boss told his employees what prices to charge. That's a baaad way to sheer a price. They said 20% off. We say that 20% off too much is still too much. We felt we were getting the staff. CK, AE, CB, DC, MC, SC, V

*
KLEINS JEWELRY
6515 Westheimer
Houston
Tel. 783-5435
M, Th 10-8
T-W, F-S 10-6

43

JEWELRY

*
OFF PREMISE—
LEVITS JEWELERS
Fondren Square
Houston
No phone listed
Sun-S 11-8

Don't stay completely Off Premise when looking for jewelry. Though their discounts didn't appear to be as large as they advertised, we did see some diamond rings marked half price at $62.50-$5000. Half price watches, also. Earrings were $10-$50 and a 7" bracelet was $10 (reg. $20). Had fairly good buys on a large quantity of Serpentine chains: 16" was $15.95 (reg. $32) and 24" was $24 (reg. $48). We dis-can't-count them as a great discounter. CK, MC, V

****
R/E KANE
ENTERPRISES
15 West 47th St.
New York City, NY
Tel. 212/246-3930

Their setup Kane not be beaten. We learned that they were able to deliver CUBIC ZIRCONIUM for $25 per diamond carat, compared to $85 elsewhere. A round CZ was $25 per diamond carat and $30 for a marquise cut. When we asked for a better deal from the crew at Kane, they mutinied. We don't blame them. This is a rock bottom deal. Send self-addressed, stamped envelope for mail order information. CK

***
WUNTCH
JEWELERS
1426 Gessner
Houston
Tel. 465-5885
Most days 10-4

These folks weren't out to Wuntch when we dropped by. Check out their jewelry, gifts and antiques. Jewelry was cut 50% off list. The antiques were excellent quality for the money. But Wuntch out for the watches—they were full retail. Antiques, like wardrobes $225, a desk $175 and old chests $150, lived up to their tags. Gold rings were $75 (reg. $150). We've a hunch you'll like Wuntch. They had irregular hours. Better to call first. CK

JUST ABOUT ANYTHING THAT'S LEGAL

*ACTIVE ELDERS—
SPRING BRANCH
YMCA
1102 Campbell Rd.
Houston
Tel. 468-1727
M-Th 8:30-7:30
F 8:30-5:30/S 9-12*

Grandpa says there are two things he could not stand to repeat. One is Aunt Lucretia's onion soup and the other is his youth. If you feel good about being senior; try this go-get-em program for those 55 years or older. They go to sporting events, dinners, movies and other fun places for reduced rates. Transportation provided by air conditioned van. Good way to get acquainted with others. Call for more information.

We found lots of good, clean fun, but very little intellectual inspiration at this disco dance club for teens. No one over 18 admitted (anything), and ID's were checked to make sure. All of our favorite soft drinks were served. Well-supervised. No communal smoking (as far as we could tell). $

"MAGIC WAY"
462 Town-Country Vil.
Houston
Tel. 465-6191
F 9:15-1/S 9-1

Peggy Burnett will do most of the things you don't have time or desire to do for $5/hr. plus .15 per mile. She will run errands, shop, select gifts, baby-sit, house sit, cook or take out the trash. We hear you will even sing us a Christmas carol, Burnett. References provided. CK

SURROGATE MOTHER
Houston
Tel. 747-6148
Call for hours

KITCHEN

Bayliwix will nix your kitchen fix. In other words, they sell every kind of equipment for the kitchen, BBQ or bar. We spotted 30-50% discounts on cutlery, stoneware, glassware, baking items, wine racks, cookware and utensils during their frequent sales. Best bet we saw was the factory seconds of white china, 50% off! CK, MC, V

**
BAYLIWIX
4836 Beechnut
Houston
Tel. 665-8454
M-F 10-6/Th 10-9
S 10-6

The Chef's Surprise was prices just a teentsy over wholesale. This chef served up everything from aprons to Woks. We saw glasses, pots, pans, plates, utensils, crocks and much more. Woks ($15.95 up), a ceramic beverage keg with spout ($19.95) and ceramic crocks ($2 up), heated up our buying thermometer. Store was spacious but cluttered. Service was a little slow. All sales final, so try not to over cook. MC, V

***
CHEF'S WAREHOUSE
6325 Westheimer
Houston
Tel. 781-7630
M-S 10-6

Pottery Plus cookware and glassware by LE CRUESET, BLANCA and STONEWARE were kitchen finds here. We saw TONS of merchandise. The best bet was the bargain area, where we glimpsed BLANCA stoneware (.50/piece), glass punchbowls ($25), cloth napkins (.79), teakwood bowls ($1.49) and a 13 piece LE CRUESET cookware set ($139). All were reduced substantially! Exchanges only. CK, MC, V

***
POTTERY PLUS
1717 S. Post Oak
Houston
Tel. 629-0950
M-F 10-9/S 10-6

LIGHTING AND LAMPS

****
**HOUSTON
CONSUMER CENTER**

See write-up under "Buying Services."

****
**LAMP
WAREHOUSE**
11450 Bissonnet
No. 316
Houston
Tel. 933-9593
M-S 10-5:30

Aladdin would have gotten a hernia trying to rub all their lamps. We found a big bunch of lamps, at very terrific prices. We loved the WESTWOOD brass table lamps ($70-$150), table/lamp combos ($29.95 up), work lamps ($10 up) and lovely brass hanging lamps ($79.99). Discounts were 40-75% off. Located in a warehouse area. CK, MC, V

SHADES 'N' SUCH
5909 Holly @ Braewick
Houston
Tel. 778-0302
M-S 11-7

This is the best, darned shady operation we've ever seen. They instruct individuals on the art of lamp shade making. Lamp bases don't wear out, but the shades do. In one evening class, they taught us how to create a professional looking custom shade at a fraction of the cost of a commercial one. A plain shade class was $35, plus material, and a pleated shade class was $45, plus material. They also had a large inventory of shade frames and rings from which to choose, and gobs of lamp parts. They also do lamp repairs. CK, V

LINENS

****
**SOUTHERN MILLS
OUTLET**

See write-up under "Bed and Bath." (Old Listings Section). Page 73.

**NR
GORDON'S
DRAPERY AND
BEDSPREADS**
5650 Beechnut
Houston
Tel. 774-6393
M-S 9-5:30

We would rather have a gourd on the head than to miss Gordon's semi-annual sales. That's the time to get great buys on DAKOTAH, SPRINGCREST, NETTLECREEK and other biggies. Their twice-a-year sales, usually in July and January, are whoopee good. Savings of 25-40% are standard on fabrics and accessories. CK, MC, V

*
LINEN CORNER
2524 Rice Ave.
Houston
Tel. 522-1300
M-S 9:30-5:30

No Corner on the Linen market. Labels were first quality—PIERRE CARDIN, ROYAL VELVET and FIELDCREST. Except for sale items, though, the prices were close to regular retail. We did spot a nifty $14.95 on a 3-pc. PIERRE CARDIN towel set and fabric shower curtains for $10. Nice selection. CK, MC, V

Their sign said, "40% off." We said, "We'd have to be if we believed the sign." FIELD-CREST, YVES ST. LAURENT, CASSINI and ANNE KLEIN were represented by. Signs like "do not touch" and "do not un-fold" greeted us, but the sales clerks didn't. Other location at 1963 W. Gray. CK

*
THE LINEN MILL
2727 Fondren
Houston
Tel. 780-0015
M-F 10-6/S 10-5

We saw many first quality items with a few irregular bedspreads, towels, custom drapes, rugs and pillows sprinkled in. Top brands like BATES, FIELDCREST, BURLINGTON and VALLEY FORGE. Don't get caught napping and miss the half-price bedspreads, with values to $90, and fitted mattress pads ($6.95-$12.95). Most merchandise was 25-50% off. Other location at Red Oak Shopping Center. CK, MC, V

**
TEXTILE OUTLET
9805 Harwin
Houston
Tel. 977-7670
M-S 10-6

MATERNITY

Tho' we didn't get to go by, we heard they were one of the neatest P.G. clothiers in town. CK

NV
MATERNITY
WEARHOUSE
OUTLET
7127 S.W. Freeway
Houston
Tel. 995-5388
T-W, F-S 10-5:30
M, Th 10-9

MEDICAL STUFF

Parents whose children are either hyper-active or learning-disabled (eye-hand coor-dination, short attention span) have banded together and are offering valuable knowl-edge to help other children. A $15 fee en-titles one to a packet, which includes a buy-ing guide of important information on safe food products. They offer a monthly news-letter with names of people who can help, plus up-to-date news regarding the latest discoveries. No one turned away because of the lack of money. Call for more info. $

*FEINGOLD
ASSOCIATION
8811 Westheimer at
Fondren, Suite 210
Houston
Tel. 780-3979
M-F 9-1*

HEALTH SCREENING
12543 West Ella
Houston
Tel. 497-0481
M-F 9-5

Having trouble standing up (even though you are a teetotaler)? Do you cough in excess of twelve hours per day? Is your tongue bluer than your eyes? You should have your Health screened. These folks beat doctor's office prices by the length of a small intestine. Test these out on your blood pressure: a complete profile (23), including blood chemistry (Dracula's collegiate minor), C.B.C. (corns, bunions and callouses?), urinalysis (so are you, fella!), EKG (not for the heartless), pulmonary (they await you, breathlessly), and an audio-visual exam (I needed a new picture tube)—all for $45. Compare to an overweight $100-$350 for a doctor's office charge. Have the tests sent to your M.D. if you're serious about getting well. Look for the vital sign on the door. CK

1960 NIGHT CLINIC
714 FM 1960 West
N. Woods Bldg., Suite U
Houston
Tel. 440-9744
M-F 6-11/S-Sun 8-11

Unlike hurts, they try harder. If you break your leg at night and can't contact your doctor, cast your fate with this clinic. Their purpose is to provide care for patients after regular office hours. If you're sick of hospital emergency room costs, you will like knowing the cost here is less and the waiting time, much less. Your doctor can refer you, but no referral needed. $

SECOND MEDICAL
OPINION HOTLINE
Tel. 800/325-6400
24 hours a day

HEW bet your life this government sponsored service will give you a second medical opinion. They operate by giving names, phone numbers and addresses of several consulting specialists. You refer your medical records to them. Most likely, additional lab tests are not needed. These doctors also accept medicare and medicaid payments. If at first you don't succeed—try for a second opinion. Call 24 hours a day.

MOTORCYCLES

Is your life going in Cycles? This is the place to Stop. Crank up 30-50% savings on parts and accessories for most makes of Japanese, European and American motorcycles. Cycle Stop is located in a 2000 sq. ft. warehouse. 90% of all parts were displayed. Points for a YAMAHA 650 were $4.95 (reg. $6.95), sprocket for a HONDA 750 was $9.95 (reg. $15.95) and a top end gasket set was $19.95 (reg. $34.95). They have been in business 11 years and are full of good advice. CK, MC, V

****
CYCLE STOP
1741 West 34
Houston
Tel. 681-0868
M-F 9-7/S 9-6

If your auto keeps breaking down, maybe you should PUCH it aside. Mopeds Only sold PUCH brand mopeds, starting at $550. Occasionally sells used ones; we saw a pre-ridden PUCH for $489. Moped service was $18/hr. plus parts. Fifteen million owners in Europe can't be all wrong. CK, MC, V

NR
MOPEDS ONLY
5549 Richmond Ave.
Houston
Tel. 782-4771
M-S 10-6

This isn't what the Lone Ranger used to say to his horse during an Indian attack. It's a neat place to have your horsepower tuned up for $12.50/cylinder. Service completed within 3 days (maximum); many dealers take two weeks. Specialize in Japanese bikes, such as HONDA, SUZUKI and KAWASAKI. $

QUICKSILVER
1210 West 12 St.
Houston
Tel. 869-6141
M-S 10-4

PARTY AND NOVELTY

The European jeweler said to his bride, as he handed her a glass of champagne, "Trinket, mine sveetie!" Well, if trinkets are your bag, grab a chance to visit this grab-bag novelty shop. Loads of cheap trinketry, stuffed animals and inflatable vinyl items. Terrific for PTA bazaars, parties or carnivals. We found we must buy in bulk form. They don't sell items singly. $

**
HOUSTON NOVELTY
COMPANY
4305 LaBranch
Houston
Tel. 527-0122
M-F 9-5

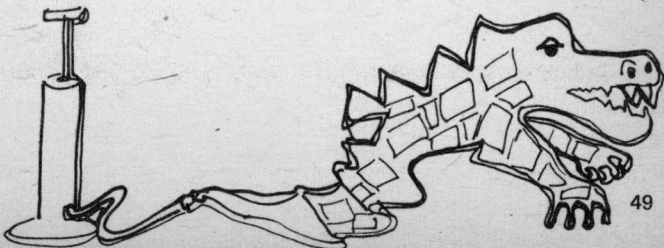

49

***
MODERN NOTION
1817 Clay
Houston
Tel. 652-5968
M-F 8:30-5

One very Modern Notion is that we're running out of oil. We discovered some party good buys, but no petroleum, at this Modern Notion. We hooked a good deal on fishing equipment and found unusual novelties for carnivals and parties. Disco key rings were $1.50 (reg. $3). Near-wholesale buys on funky jewelry, TIMEX watches, toys and sporting goods. Merchandise was arranged nicely in cases or on pegboard displays. They got our vote at this League of Notions. CK

PETS

ANIMAL BIRTH
CONTROL CENTER
908 E. Temple
Houston
Tel. 864-0395
By appt. only

Birth control devices available here for animal "lovers"! Low cost spay and neuter clinic for your amorous animal. Our female cat went down, spay-ed the day for only $15 and went out on the town that very night. CK

ANIMAL
EMERGENCY CLINIC
8921 Katy
Houston
Tel. 932-9589
Weeknights 6:30-7 a.m.
S 12:30 p.m. to 7 a.m.

If your pet pig pulls a hamstring, call the Animal Emergency Clinic for immediate information. They'll suggest treatment—wrap in towel, brace leg, etc.—to be performed while on the way to their nearest clinic. It's emergency care only, and it is provided by the Southwest Veterinary Community. They charged $23 plus treatment and don't keep pets overnight. Other locations and phone numbers: 610 Loop Area—4676 Beechnut, 661-0150; North Harris County—14232 W. Montgomery Rd., 444-0137; South East Area—9331 Gulf Freeway, 941-4530; South West Area—6361 Westheimer, 783-4690. CK, MC, V

***
AQUAWORLD NO. 1
10045 Long Point
Houston
Tel. 464-5093
M-F 11-7/Sun 11-6

Nothing fishy here! Just good prices on a wide selection of fish and fish supplies. An aquarium set-up (10 gal.) with tank, pump, filter, charcoal, floss and tubing was $5.99. Fifty pounds of gravel was $2.59. Jaws never had it so good. Save a few fin with buys on Comets ($1/15), Rosie Barb ($1/2), Blushing Angel ($1/2) and Rainbow Shark (.99/ea.). A great price "scale". $

THE CITIZENS ANIMAL PROTECTION SERVICE IS ALL C.A.P.S. WITH US. They're a non-profit adoption service for dogs and cats. An excellent way to secure a pet with a clean bill of health. Pets are neutered or spayed and have received all their shots. The adoption fee starts at $20 and is tax deductible. $

C.A.P.S.
(Citizens Animal
Protection Service)
P.O. Box 27088
Houston
Tel. 651-1875
      651-0074
Call for hours

They advertised, "Everything for the wild bird enthusiast." We have never met a wild one. Some were a bit obsessed, but who isn't. We found BUSHNELL binoculars $42.50-$442.50 and spotting scopes $49.95 and up. Prices were a tweet 25% off. We also seed bird feeders, books, records, tapes, baths, bird houses. Window viewers were $5.95. Migrate to the old house in the Montrose area and peck out a painting or print $15-$500. It was birdie interesting. CK

**
**THE CHICKADEE &
NATURALIST
EMPORIUM**
702 Marshall St.
Houston
Tel. 528-0139
W-S—Call for hours

You might want to "bow" out when you whiff the animal food odor, but you'll "wow" at the big merchandise selection. Not a pet shop, but a supply house for pet supplies and all animal foods. Foods came fresh or frozen (lots of ground beef). Hundreds of books about animals, plus lotsa supplies, such as leashes, flea collars, grooming equipment, cat stands and humming bird feeders. Scents for hunters. CK

***
**KENNEL TOWN PET
SHOP AND SUPPLIES**
1302 West Gray
Houston
Tel. 522-3621
T-F 9-5/S 9-2

If it's to bee or not to bee, and that is the question you've been asking yourself, then here's the shake down: $100 for beginner set equipment and about $25 for bees to stock. Won't Koska much. CK

NV
**KOSKA BEE
SUPPLIES**
915 Boundry
Houston
Tel. 226-8311
M-F 7:30-5

It's 10 o'clock. Do you know where your kitty is? If not, you might need to take it to the Neuter Clinic. Or if your dog can't stand the heat, cool it with their one day service—in by 8:00, off by 4:00. Cats spayed $15 or neutered $8; dogs spayed ($20 under 30 lb.—$25-30 over 30 lb.), neutered $15-$25. Good prices on vaccinations, also. CK

NEUTER CORP.
ANIMAL CONTROL
CLINIC INC.
4520 Katy Fwy.
Houston
Tel. 868-2375
T-F 6:30-6/S 7:30-5

PHOTOGRAPHY

**NR
PHOTOGRAPHIC
RENTAL SERVICES**
5863 Bissonnet
Houston
Tel. 667-9267
Call for hours

PRS will lense you a camera or projector for a film-sy price. Zoom in with CANON, NIKON, PENTAX and VIVITAR cameras or focus on the deals for lenses (24-260 power). Then project your talents on the silver screen with a 8mm or 16mm projector. Take a shot at it! $

PLANTS

*
**ANN'S WHOLESALE
NURSERY INC.**
22 mi. W of Hwy. 6 on
FM 1093 (Westheimer)
Simonton
Tel. 346-1442
M-S 9-5

We would have had to be out of our tree not to drop in. They petal ferns, African violets, bromeliads and begonias, Ruby! Large selection of plants made the trip worthwhile—we didn't want to leaf. We got bushed, touring their wide selection. $

**NR
ECO WORM
PRODUCTS**
6108 Brittmore Road
Houston
Tel. 466-1208
M-F 9-6/S 9-12

Eco Worm produces a natural fertilizer product that is organically great! The fertilizer, made from worm castings (worm's No. 2) is labeled SUPER STUFF—a product originated in Houston. The straight poop is that the castings produce one of the world's richest, natural, organic fertilizers. With SUPER STUFF'S super success, worm farms have been cropping up nationwide to feed this earthworm mania. $

**
MUNSON NURSERY
18920 North Fwy.
Houston
Tel. 353-2005
M-S 8:30-6/Sun 9-6

We loved these mulch-kins. Best buy was pine bark mulch at 25-30% off. Graded in fine, medium and large (cordwood?). We paid the same price last year—$1.50/bag and $12/10 bags! Plants and pottery weren't discounted mulch overall. Lots of statues, fountains and wrought iron for the garden. CK

*
PLANTS N THINGS
2841 Fondren
Houston
Tel. 782-2440
M-F 10-7/S 9:30-6
Sun 1-6

Jeepers, peepers where'd you get those creepers? P & T was full of plants, ceramics, pottery, figurines and baskets, all claiming to be half price! But jeepers, we felt like their discounts were as small as their tiny shop. We couldn't find the 50% off they advertised. You might want to peep elsewhere before buying. CK, MC, V

The forest formula at Redwood Chemical called for one part selection, one part low prices and one part good service. They handled insecticides and swimming pool supplies at wholesale prices. We saw a pool skimmer for $8, one pound SPECTRACIDE insect dust for $2.29, tile cleaner—one quart for $4.25 and 2 pounds of pool stabilizer for $6. It's probably where your neighborhood exterminator and pool cleaner pick up their supplies. $

***
REDWOOD CHEMICAL
1215 Jackson
Houston
Tel. 658-0231
M-F 7:30-5

Hi, tall, green and handsome. We had heard green stuff was the root of all evil. Not so, at Tall Plants. Prices on large scheffleras $59.95, corn plants $19.95-$129, philodendrons $4.95 and big palms $29.95 and up were less than sinful. They said wholesale—we said not quite. Delivery costs stretched to $25 for ten mile radius (we carried ours home ourselves). MC, V

**
TALL PLANTS
9191 Katy Fwy.
Houston
Tel. 464-9671
M-S 10-6/Sun 1-5

PORCELAIN REPAIR

Rub-a-dub-dub, Norman Gulledge will do a job on your tub. 21 years experience on bathtub resurfacing. It takes him at least 72 hours to do the job right (a little at a time). Usually takes three visits to your home, because he includes an interliner during the process so that the finished job will last. Resurfaces or repairs chips of ceramic tile, porcelain, fiberglass, cultured marble and china. Your rubber ducky will marble at the finish. Cost was $155 plus $10 more for out of town. Ah, there's the rub, but cheaper than a new tub. CK

LECTROGLAZ
Houston
Tel. 645-3909
Call for appt.

PRINTERS

Paupers are treated like prints at Budget. Excellent prices on letterheads, business forms, announcements and stationery. Photo copies were still only .05, and business cards were $14.95/1000! $

***
BUDGET PRINT CENTER
10302-A Harwin
Houston
Tel. 666-0008
M-F 8:30-5:30

*
**SOUTHWEST
RECORD AND TAPE
CO.**
5757 Westheimer
Houston
Tel. 780-7427
M-S 11-10

There won't be any records set for discounts here, but we did find a "head-y" collection of incense, PLAYBOY greeting cards, funky jewelry and necklaces. Saw albums as low as $1.50 and others for $10 (reg. $12.95). They sold drug paraphernalia, such as cocaine test sets and pipes, which doesn't mean they condone illicit drug use, but merely that they want to make a few bucks off those who do. Other location at 14011 Memorial Drive. $

RECYCLE

*BODNER METAL
AND IRON CORP.*
3660 Schalker
Houston
Tel. 223-1148
Call for hours

Howdy, Bodner! These folks buy scrap metal. Get rid of that ole clunker at the rate of $50/ton of steel. They specialize in industrial accounts, but will consider individuals.

DIAL RE-CYCLING
800/223-6830

You'll be glad you used Dial! So will your whole family when you turn in aluminum items at the rate of .20/lb. They have 2200 sites across the country, with a special 24-hour hotline. Sponsored by the Aluminum Association.

*HOUSTON
DISTRIBUTING
COMPANY*
2121 Edwards
Houston
Tel. 864-4424
M-F 8:30-2:30

Foiled again, but no curses. Foil plates, frozen food containers, cans, trays or any type of aluminum bring .20/lb. from these folks. That's about 23 cans/lb. We'll drink to that. They match the amount of money paid to you and give it to the U.S. Olympic team.

*NAT'L. BEVERAGE
RECYCLING PLANT*
1512-1516 Live Oak
Houston
Tel. 691-1171
M-F 9-3

If you can do a clean can-can, they'll pay you .17-.21/lb. for them. But they must be clean. If you call for current prices, we hope you don't get the woman we did. She didn't want to be bothered. Try Houston Distributing Co. They do.

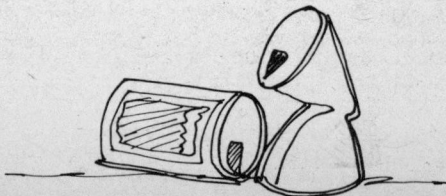

A paper chase is going on at 47 N. Hamilton. They're really into yesterday's news, and pay $1/100 lbs. for newspaper, .50/100 lbs. for old corrugated boxes, $4/100 lbs. for computer paper and $5/100 lbs. for IBM tabs. Yesterday's news can buy tomorrow's newspapers!

*SUNSET FIBRE
OF HOUSTON*
47 N. Hamilton
Houston
Tel. 224-9317
M-F 8-9/S 8-11:30

REMODELING

Crafty old Clark is a master carpenter. He is available for odd jobs on even days and even works on odd days. He does all kinds of carpenter work—from replacing shingles to putting on siding to nailing steps together. He hits the nail on the head. CK

CLARK BROWN
Houston
Tel. 946-8440
      646-8039
Call for hours

Have you barbequed your kitchen? Are you having glass pains? Call Ralph. He has about 20 handy guys working for him. Ralph gives free estimates for almost any type of home repair. Minimum charge is $29. This included trip fee $15 and one hour $14/hr. CK, MC, V

HOUSTON HANDY MAN, INC.
Houston
Tel. 449-3460
Call for hours

RESALE SHOP

Sam used to go with a debutante who was so fat she had to have a 2nd Debut, just to come out all the way. The 2nd Debut on Westheimer featured clothes and accessories, such as children's T-shirts for $1, boy's suits, women's dresses (in excellent condition) for $10-$30 and maternity clothes for $8-$14. We spotted a super array of designer shoes and clothes. They also had antiques, jewelry and bric-a-brac. Much of their merchandise was on consignment. CK, MC, V

***
2ND DEBUT RESALE SHOP
10930 Westheimer
Houston
Tel. 782-8227
M-S 10-6

55

ROACHICIDE

NR
ROACH PRUFE
SALES
1494 Wilcrest
Houston
Tel. 780-7755
M-F 10-6/S 9-5

Are your roaches thriving on that store bought stuff? Try ROACH PRUFE. Effective due to electrostatically charged, reconstituted boric acid. It's carried back into the walls on their legs where it kills their shy friends, too. Available only by mail. Price quoted was $7.95 plus $1.50 handling for one lb.; enough for nine rooms. Clip your roach problems! CK

SCHOOLS

CLASS FACTORY
5326 W. Bellfort
Suite 210
Houston
Tel. 721-2230
M-F 9-5

We thought a class factory was one with Beethoven on the Muzak and designer toilet paper in the John. Not here. This was a school with an unusual curriculum. Phone to be put on their mailing list. Classes in the past have included: Suddenly Single $15, Writing Resumes That Work $12, Disco Dance $8, Disco Tour $5, Fishing $12, Gourmet Wine and Cheese Tasting $7 and Japanese Flower Arranging $6. Good way to meet people with similar interests.

SHOE REPAIR

HOUSTON SHOE
HOSPITAL
5215 Kirby Dr.
Houston
Tel. 528-6208
M-F 7-6/S 7-3

Down in the heels? Sole-sick? Shoes ready for Boot Hill? They rebuild old shoes and boots like new again. Rebuilt boots were $24.95/pr., men's shoes were $16.95/pr. and ladies' shoes were $10.95/pr. They do over a quarter million shoes per year, operating out of Nantucket Cleaners. Also do golf and tennis shoes. Check directory for other locations. MC, V

SHOES

NV
OK PAWN AND
SALVAGE
613 Sam Houston
Huntsville, TX 77340

Up to now, we've heard of only one person who could walk on water. Now, you can too! It's OK, though. These are waterfilled innersoles. They retail for less than $5. Inchoir for more info. $

56

SMOKES

Smoke gets in your pies, and in your breakfast, lunch and supper! Lew Rothman at J-R Tobacco in New York has cigars so cheap you can pollute for pennies from dawn 'til dusk. They'll stench your thirst for paltry puffing. She says they are the nation's leading mail order purveyor of cigars—the cheroot source for postal panatelas. We compared local stogie store's prices and found J-R's savings to be 25-50% off. They stocked many brands.

****
J-R TOBACCO
108 West 45th St.
New York, NY 10026
Toll free 800-431-2380

See write-up under "Buying Services."

****
**HOUSTON
CONSUMER CENTER**

SPIRITS

Quit wining about the price of booze and start making your own. De Falco offered starter kits for $14.95/gal. with concentrate and $29.95/5 gal. with concentrate. White wines take six months, and red wines as much as a year, but never fear—beer makers were $7.95-$19.95 and processing time was much shorter. Amaretto, Galiano, Drambuie, Tia Maria and Kahlua mixes were $2.99. We enjoyed our cordial visit. CK

NR
**DE FALCO WINE
CELLARS**
2435 University
Houston
Tel. 523-8154
M-S 10-6

It's hard to bar these folks from a successful party. They are a complete liquor store. Their prices are marked up 18%, rather than the "status quo" of 25%. They offer a very professional bartending service "par excellence". The service was $20/hr. with an additional discount if the liquor was ordered from them. Watch for second location. CK, MC, SC, V

MR. DRINK
9220 Richmond Ave.
Houston
Tel. 780-4839
M-S 10-9

Huge case discounts, but good single jug prices, too. We saw J.W. DANT for $6.75/qt., DEWAR'S for $10.15/qt., BACARDI rum for $5.89/qt. and champagne for $3.45. Because they are so low on their prices, they don't want your credit card business. CK

***
**SPEC'S LIQUOR
WAREHOUSE**
2410 Smith
Houston
Tel. 528-8786
M-S 10-9

**

TUCK'S TAP-A-KEG
10902 Shadowood
Houston
Tel. 467-8326
Call for hours

My friend Harold can Tuck beer away by the gallon! I suds-gested he buy it by the keg and save. Excellent for parties. He found large (15½ gal.) and pony (8 gal.) kegs. COORS was $47.63 (large) and $31 (pony), and prices on other brands varied slightly. Prices included 100 cups (10 oz.), 50 lbs. of ice and taxes. The large keg held 296 servings (before Harold got ahold of it). Large savings for large consumers. Three day limit for possession of keg. $50 deposit. CK

SPORTING GOODS AND BADS

**

KENLEE'S LOCKED IN SPORTS
9703 Katy Fwy.
Houston
Tel. 461-3134
M-S 9-6

Scuba-do-be-do. Kenlee's sells scuba gear, services and test equipment. They schedule trips and teach classes. Scuba classes were $125 (for an 18 hour course). They advertised "25% off." We saw prices that seemed to be consistent with that claim. Call for more information. Check directory for other locations. $

**

THE SPORTS STOP
10976 Westheimer
Houston
Tel. 780-9286
M-F 10-7/S 10-6

You say your bike has become a shiftless hulk? Send it to The Sports Shop for a basic tune-up ($12.50 plus parts). Shop was filled with sporting equipment, such as DUNLOP tennis balls $2.19, strap-on roller skates $49.95, men's and women's roller skates $50-$89.95, athletic shoes, clothing and RALEIGH bikes. Ex-chain-ges accepted. CK, MC, SC, V

TELEPHONES

EASTERN ONION
Houston
Tel. 680-1975
M-F 8-6/S 10:30-2:30

This onion brought tears of laughter to our eyes. We got to choose from 40 songs that applied to birthdays, anniversaries, good-byes, promotions, retirement and even divorces! The delivery person showed up in a red hat/jacket, black pants uniform with a mechanical monkey (trade-mark) and gag gifts; the rest has to be seen to be believed. Prices started at $27 with one week notice required most of the time. MC, V

Have lots of blood relatives in Transylvania? Take the bite out of waiting for overseas information to look up numbers; stake a claim to an international phone book (any country) from Ma Bell. Average cost is $6/book and it takes about two weeks to receive it. $

HOUSTON TELEPHONE
To contact your local business office see the front pages of white pages.
M-F 9-5

LDS is a long distance telephone service that saves 40% on your calls to and from San Antonio, Houston, Dallas, Fort Worth, Austin and Corpus Christi. To make a call, dial their telephone number. One of their operators will answer. Give her your account number, the city and telephone number you want to call. It's that simple. There is a monthly service charge of $10/mo. (home) and $50 (business). $

LDS, INC.
(Long Distance Services)
Houston
Tel. 225-9052
M-S 8-10

Enter the calls of antiquity. Send for catalog of authenic, conventionally made antique telephones. They also have parts for old phones. A big selection. $

PHONES UNLIMITED
P.O. Box 61146
Houston, TX 77208

These folks should get the no-Bell prize for cheapness. SPC offers an alternative to standard long distance service provided by the telephone company. It can result in substantial savings on your monthly long distance bill. Called "SPRINT", the service is provided by SPCommunications Co. (a subsidiary of the Southern Pacific Company). While you can't reach the entire country with SPRINT, the service does cover most major metropolitan areas and their suburbs and it is expanding rapidly. Depending on the type of call (time of day, distance, etc.) savings over Ma Bell's rates range from 25-85%. No additional equipment needed and there are no extra lines or hook up fees required. $

SPCOMMUNICATIONS
7171 Harwin, Suite 210
Houston
Tel. 974-4444
M-F 8:30-5:30

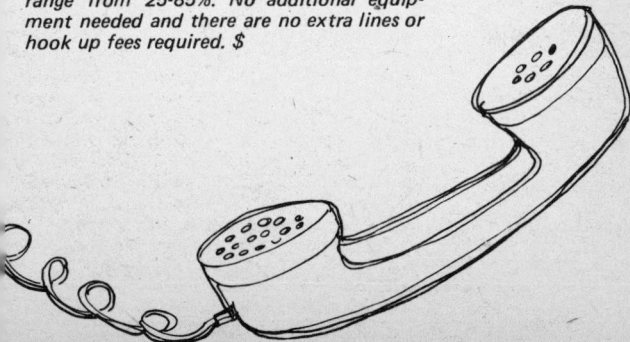

TRANSPORTATION

COMMUTAIR'S
Hwy. 6 near Sugarland
Houston
Tel. 491-3111
      645-1030
5:10 a.m.-10:05 p.m.

Rise above it all. This will save you plenty of time, but not a dime (unless your car gets one mile per gallon). Try Commutair's 20 minute commuter flights from Hull Field to Intercontinental and Hobby, for $20 each way. Eleven flights daily starting 5:55 a.m.—9 p.m. Flights require three day reservation and carry only eight passengers. Free parking. $

WE DRIVE, INC.
2222 Westerland
No. 238
Houston
Tel. 785-8402
M-F 9-5

Tired of paying an arm and leg for a taxi to the airport, or leaving your auto there for weeks on end? We Drive has an economical solution. They'll chauffeur you (and friends) to the airport for a $15 flat rate using your car, and pick you up when you return. Notify them of your schedule and they'll make the arrangements. Excellent for sporting and entertainment events. Call for more information. $

TV REPAIR

NR
WHOLESALE TV
1010 Stering
Houston
Tel. 496-5098
Call for hours

These guys came to our house, fixed our set for $5 plus parts (another $63). The cheapest competitive estimate was $105, and we had to take the set into the shop. We expect you had better hurry. They won't be able to last forever at these prices. Allow three days for service. $

WALLCOVERINGS

*
THE WALLPAPER
SHOPPE
9440 Old Katy Road
Houston
Tel. 461-5126
M-F 9-5

The trouble with wallpaper is that the paster usually ends up being the pastee. If you don't care, drop by The Wallpaper Shoppe. When we were there, they had over 700 books from which to choose, featuring vinyl, mylar, grasscloth, textures and handcrafted prints. We saw several designer lines among the samples. They allowed books to be checked out over night. They also had upholstery fabrics, draperies, bedspreads, mini-blinds, wovenwoods and accessories. CK, MC, V

WONDERFUL WAX

What is tall, white and burns at both ends? No, it isn't a big Anglo after a jalapeno eating contest. It's a candle, of course. We discovered lotsa beautiful candles at 50% off. The candles were seconds, but you could have fooled us. The flaws were very hard to detect. We saw a great selection of Texas style candles—Texas shaped maps $3.25, Texas oil derricks $7, and armadillos $3.25. CK

****
CANDLEIGN, INC.
7609 Boone Road
Houston
Tel. 495-1767
M-S 9-5

WEIRD, ETC.

Get listed with these folks for $20. They will send you a list of member's profiles (in code). Get acquainted through the mail. Singles only. Proper only. Serious only. CK

NR
BIBLIOBUFFS
Box 530
Ingram, TX 78025

Connie's cups sized up to a D-lightful party experience. She personalized our styrofoam cups with our own design. Minimum order was 250 for $33.95/9 oz., $39.95/14 oz. and $49.95/16 oz. She also personalized matchbooks. MC, V

NR
CONNIE'S CRAZY CUPS
3901 Richmond
Houston
Tel. 629-0745
M-F 10-6/S 10-3

We crepe to Suzette's window one day and found some revealing sights: SUZETTE and ARTEX labels featuring clothes for the "swinging crowd". Teacup candy bras and bikini candy panties $15/ea. Nothing was plain vanilla. Sexy lingerie $10 and up and disco dresses $20-$80. No discounts on price, but don't discount the results. CK, MC, SC, V

NR
SUZETTE'S
6516 Westheimer
Houston
Tel. 781-4811
M-S 9-6

WESTERN STUFF

Wow! They actually permit their customers to purchase a five cent piece of cardboard for $10. For $10/yr., we were told we could buy a discount card entitling us to 10% off on all merchandise, except sale items. Whoopee? CK, DC, MC, SC, V

*
BIG IRON WESTERN WEAR
11012 Airline
Houston
Tel. 445-1238
M-S 10-8

**
BLINDS AND THINGS
Houston
Tel. 495-6918
By appt. only

This blind man will come to your home to see what your window covering needs are. BALI and LEVELOR mini-blinds were 30-40% off. Also saw wovenwoods with valences. Blinds were made to order. Call ahead for address or appointment. CK

*
DECORATING DEN
Woodlands
Houston
Tel. 367-3842
Call for hours

Woodn't wovenwoods look good in your home? The Decorative Den offered vertical wovenwoods at 20% off. They operated from vans instead of a store front and measured and installed in our home. We thought it was vantastic. Their motto is, "Important decisions should be made at home." No charge for estimates. $

****
HOUSTON CONSUMER CENTER

See write-up under "Buying Services."

****
INTERIOR FABRICS
3047 Fondren
Houston
Tel. 789-9222
M-F 9-5/S 10-4

Go three blocks south of Westheimer to find hundreds of designs from leading fabric houses including BURLINGTON, BLOOMCRAFT, COHAMA, LA FRANCE, WAMSUTTA, SCHUMACHER and WAVERLY. Save 50% and more on drapery fabric ($1.99-$3.99/yd., reg. to $8/yd.), upholstery fabric ($5.99-$9.99/yd., reg. to $25/yd.). Velvet, crewel, chintz, satin, suede, moire, jacquard, canvas—you name it. Affiliated with the very successful Cutting Corners in Dallas/Fort Worth. CK, MC

NR
JIMMY'S UPHOLSTERY AND DRAPERY SHOP
7353 Fence
Houston
Tel. 631-7861
M-F 8-4:30

Jimmy doesn't work for peanuts, but he's still pretty reasonable. We saw HERCULON drapes at 40% off. Jimmy gave free estimates, but said it would take a while for him to get to a customer. As Orson Welles nearly said in his wine commercial, "We pick no drape before its time". Also does upholstery. Location is hard to find. Call for directions. CK

**
THE PAPERED WALL
5901-K Westheimer
Houston
Tel. 789-6823
M-F 10-6/S 10:30-4

Whether you want mini-blinds or just a few, we found that a good place to get them was The Papered Wall. They offered 40% discounts on them, with an additional 10% off for ten blinds or more. We also found 30% off on verticals and 35% off on wovenwoods. Top labels like DELMAR, BAMBOO, ABBOT, LEVELOR and BALI blind-ed us to any other choice. They also had wallpaper and carpet. CK

NIFTY NUMBERS

Gas
ENTEX *(You light up my wife.)*   659-2111

Electricity
Houston Lighting and Power Company
(This is the current number.)   228-9711

Water
City of Houston *(They turned on my tap, Danzer.)*   224-2500

Telephone
Southwestern Bell *(Take it or leave it.)*   237-7811

Medical Assistance
Doctors' Referral Service *(HELP!!)*   790-1838
Dental Referral Service *(help.)*   790-9690
Optometric Referral Service *(Would you read
the number for me, please?)*   695-4105

Legal Assistance
Gulf Coast Legal Foundation *(Suits me.)*   225-0321
Houston Bar Association *(Guild-y.)*   222-1441

Emergency Numbers
Ambulance, Emergency only *(We deliver.)*   222-3434
Fire *(Follows, "Ready, aim.")*   227-2323
Police *(Don't call us. We'll call you.)*   222-3131

Other Miscellaneous Numbers

Better Business Bureau *(What can I do with half a
swimming pool?)*   654-1122
Chamber of Commerce *(Dallas who?)*   651-1313
Citizenship *(What's alien you?)*   226-4251
City Hall *(Wanna fight?)*   222-3011

City Planning Commission *(Nobody's perfect.)*   222-3261
Dept. of Human Resources *(I'll take four shorts,
one medium and two talls.)*   526-3531
Harris County Flood Control *(Flood? What flood?)*   221-5162
Houston Credit Bureau *(So what if I went bankrupt?
That was eight whole months ago!)*   652-3434

Internal Revenue *(Stick 'em up!)*   965-0440
Social Security *(How to be confident at parties?)*   524-4781
Texas Highway Department *(The road gang.)*   869-4571
VA (Veteran's Administration)
(Invite 'em over for S.O.S.)   664-4664

OLD FRIENDS,
SOME TRIED AND TRUE,
SOME TRIED AND BOO.

TEN COMMANDMENTS FOR AUCTION BUYING
or
Now That You've Bought the Golden Calf
How Do You Get It Home?

I   Thou shalt preview the merchandise before bidding.

II   Thou shalt worship no false auctioneers, but check out their local reputation.

III   Thou shalt not bid in vain, or bid over retail to beat that smart aleck down the aisle.

IV   Thou shalt sit on both hands until ready to bid, lest returning from the john, you find that you have bought it.

V   Thou shalt not yell to bid—a nod will do.

VI   Thou shalt not bid on any item too big for the back of your car or motorcycle.

VII   Thou shalt honor thy mother-in-law, but not sit with her.

VIII   Thou shalt not be a crybaby if what you buy isn't what you expected.

IX   Remember the lot number. If you like the antique commode, chances are you'll love the bed—if the lot numbers are the same.

X   Thou shalt not covet comfort, but relax and enjoy the atmosphere . . . even unto the hard folding chairs.

OLD LISTINGS UPDATE

ANIMAL LOVERS

*
SPCA
519 Studemont
Houston
Tel. 869-8227
M-S 9-5/Sun 1-5

Even Hard Hearted Hannah wouldn't be able to say no to these adorable puppies $20 and kittens $10. Full grown dogs start at $20, and cats are the same price. All shots included in these prices. CK

ANTIQUES, AUCTIONS, COLLECTIBLES

*
A-1 ANTIQUES
1905 S. Shaver
Pasadena
Tel. 473-0373
S nite auctions 7 PM

Going once, going twice, GONE! A-1 Antiques put great antiques on the auction block and we put our money on the line. Offered approximately 300 items every Saturday night with sneak preview viewing time on Friday from 4-9 PM, and on Saturday from 11-7. The oldest auction business in Texas, this store was high on quality and prices. CK

**
THE APPLE BOX
2391 Calder
Beaumont
Tel. 832-1247
M-S 10-5

This store was in apple pie order. Located in an old seven room house, each room displayed items for sale which you'd usually find in that particular room of your home. The kitchen held dishes, pots and pans and just guess where we found a dining room table for sale? You got it! The dining room. The merchandise, new and old, was priced just right with no bad apples in sight. CK, MC, V

***
THE BOARDING HOUSE
1653 Blalock
Houston
Tel. 461-1173
M-S 9:30-5/S 10:30-4

We didn't find any rooms for rent at The Boarding House, but the English and Austrian antiques could stay over at our house any time. We had to reach for the smelling salts when we saw fainting couches and cupboards in the $400-$800 price range. With everything else they had to offer, we didn't even care that the jewelry selection had apparently taken lodging elsewhere. CK, AE, MC, SC, V

This is one tea leaf we had trouble reading! Owned by four ladies who stock everything from furniture to cream bottles, this store was small on space but offered some off the wall charm. We spotted a Victorian server for $400. We also saw some great brass candlestick holders. CK

*
THE BRASS TEA
LEAF
2356 Bissonnet
Houston
Tel. 527-0841
M-F 10-4

When we saw Bristol's goodies, we bristled with anticipation. Jerry McClellan, the auctioneer, had gavel, would travel. When he's at home, the historical goodies that are sold across his auction block will dazzle you. Antiques and other old stuff from England, Austria and America were on display in quantities too large to ignore. The coffee and entertainment at the Saturday auctions was free, but the merchandise was the real show. When we were there, we saw a band wagon with music box, English taxis horns and a few original gypsy wagons. From grandfather clocks to pianos, it was all there for the bidding. CK

****
BRISTOL ANTIQUES,
LTD.
1302 South Broadway
La Porte
Tel. 471-1313
    862-7579
S sale 7 PM
S inspection noon-7

If great architecture lives on, then Bruce Adkins Architectural Antiques may be around for awhile. If not, who knows? Large selection of expensive old mantels, doors of every size, hardware, furniture and light fixtures. Great variety, but unfortunately that was not the spice of our lives—bargains were. Historical looks, but all at new inflationary prices. CK

*
BRUCE ADKINS
ARCHITECTURAL
ANTIQUES
3515 Fannin
Houston
Tel. 522-6547
M-F 9-5/S 9-4

No clothes but plenty of clutter prevailed here. More of a gift shop, with no real antiques (mainly stuff from the 30's and 40's). 50% of store's stock was on consignment. Lots of knick-knacks for those who have a knack for knicks. CK, MC, V

*
CLOTHES 'N'
CLUTTER
2421 Sunset Blvd.
Houston
Tel. 529-9501
T-F 11-6/S 11-4

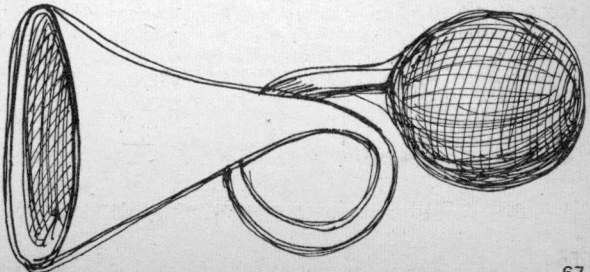

ANTIQUES, AUCTIONS, COLLECTIBLES

***
DOT'S GLASS AND TRASH SHOP
219 N. Main St.
Baytown
Tel. 427-7752
M-S 10-4

We dashed to Dot's for glass and trash. Known as the "Junk Lady", Dot had been spending her time organizing her real antiques when we dropped by to see her. Her private collection of dolls, linens and jewelry were in perfect condition, unlike some of her other items. Primitive kitchen wares, furniture, trunks, etc., were all found at Dot's and she was more than willing to talk price or anything else. (An uncomparable gift of gab!) $

**
FORGET-ME-NOT ANTIQUES
957 Brittmore
Houston
Tel. 468-3551
T-S 10-5

We couldn't pick a bouquet of bargains at Forget-Me-Not Antiques, since they wouldn't soft-petal their prices. We saw a Victorian high back bed for $300. Most of their strictly American furniture was oak and walnut. Forget-you-not to ask about the items stored out in the garage. Could be a better bargain remembered out there. CK

***
FURNITURE MKT.
7201 Chimney Rock
Bellaire
Tel. 665-7090
T-S 10-5

Some stuff at this Market was cheaper by the pound than hamburger. This store had bargains galore. For years, the owners habit of collecting and trading with friends and neighbors has made this store tops on our list. An oak dresser with velvet lining for $150 had us reaching for our cash and an oak buffet for $90 made us wish we'd brought more. The quality and prices made shopping here a delight. CK, MC, V

**
HELEN'S OF PASADENA
1922 Strawberry
Pasadena
Tel. 477-1095
Tea Room M-S 11-3
Gift M-S 10-5

The antiques were delectable, but the homemade bread, quiche, and spiced tea were delicious! This antique/tea shop had a different approach (through our stomachs!) to selling antiques. We could have stayed forever sampling all their heavenly delights, but our waist line couldn't take the strain. CK, MC, V

*
JUDY COON'S ANTIQUES & GIFTS
25269 FM 2100
Hufsmith
Tel. 324-1745
T-S 10-4

Oh, say, Coon you see any cheap stuff for me? A little. We went a-wandering through the old curio cabinets, pictures, vases, glassware, chairs and stained glass windows $42-$150. TIFFANY lamps (20 year old reproductions) were lighting up our world at $175-$525. Nice selection. CK

68

We could have used some Lyn-amint to rub on our neck after looking high and low at their big selection. This store didn't overwhelm us with warmth, but neither does Paul Newman and he's not so bad. Their specialty was 18th century furniture. We saw some handmade silk flowers from Germany .50-$6 and lots of complete sets of 19th century china. CK

*
LYN'S ANTIQUES
2579 Calder Ave.
Beaumont
Tel. 835-1927 (shop)
        892-3086 (home)
M-F 9:30-5/S 10-4

A lot of oldies and goodies here but information on the store was hard to come by. (Sorry we asked!) Offered American oak furniture, dolls and pillows, to name a few. Marked merchandise is for sale. No price, no sale. Maybe they should have refinished their attitude toward shoppers when they were refinishing some of their goods. MC, V

*
**OLDIES BUT
GOODIES ANTIQUES**
912 Yale
Houston
Tel. 869-1015
M-S 10-5

We thought we heard AVON calling, but it was actually JIM BEAM. Loads of these type of bottles (and more) available here. The collections of pitchers and depression glass were the real eye catchers, with dressers and mirrors deserving a second glance. The parking wasn't great, but the friendly atmosphere made it worth getting in a tight spot. CK

*
R & E ANTIQUES
1104 N. Cleveland
Dayton
Tel. 258-5694
T-F 10-5/S 10-4

We were Even-Steven, Reeves, when we left your super store. We got by cheaply on old furniture. Greater part of the furniture was from the 1920's. If you're handy, check out their frames of furniture and do your own thing. A china cabinet was quite a dish, and they had plenty priced from $400-$2200. A second store at 2401 Taft holds more. CK, MC, V

***
**REEVES FURNITURE
COMPANY**
4901 Washington
Houston
Tel. 869-9224
M-S 9:30-6

If what you're hoping to find is the real thing, check out the Coca Cola trays at Sid's $6. Lots of brass items and brass lamps threw out a real beacon to these weary shoppers. A wrought iron table with marble top for $125 was a steal of a deal, and a wood goose for $29 made us take another gander. CK, MC, V

**
**SID'S ANTIQUES
AND GIFTS**
I-10 at Addicks
Addicks
Tel. 493-1040
Sun-S 11-5
Some F, S nights

THE STRIP SHOP
1653 Blalock
Houston
Tel. 461-0863
M-S 9-5

If Aunt Beatrice says she took it all off at The Strip Shop, don't call a cop. This store offered super furniture stripping, refinishing and caning service. Free advice on special problems such as water stains. If you do your own refinishing, this store has supplies to help with prices that needn't be covered up. CK

*
TRASH AND
TREASURE
1716 Westheimer
Houston
Tel. 522-7415
     522-5601
M-F 8-4/S 8-3

At first glance we thought this store was the city dump working under an alias, but a little looking uncovered some of the treasure. A cut glass water pitcher $650 and a high wheeler bicycle $750 were just some of the finds. Everything was stacked up to the ceiling and we had some trouble finding the ins and outs of the place (not too many doors, some shutters). CK

NR
UNITED STATES
TREASURY SERVICE
Houston
Tel. 921-2882
Annual Fall Auction

We eagerly attended, hoping we could pick up some used $100 bills for pennies, but found such items as heavy machinery, furniture, 44 bags of chestnut extract, 20 bags of swimming goggles, five boxes of soccer balls and doll heads (they auctioned off the bodies last year). The auction is held only once a year. Worth going to, just to see the weird stuff. $

APPLIANCES

*
CONN'S
195 N. 11th St.
Beaumont
Tel. 838-6504
M-F 8-8/S 8-6

This store's deal was no Conn job! If we could find lower price elsewhere, all we had to do was let them know and they'd refund the difference. Good savings on AMANA, WESTINGHOUSE, MAYTAG, G.E., MAG-NAVOX and FRIGIDAIRE. They carried loads of appliances and we loved having them as a conn-ection to good bargains. CK, MC, V

****
HOUSTON
CONSUMER CENTER

See write-up under "Buying Services." (New Listings Section)

We were Star-tled at Stars; the deals were that good. This was where the stars came out—KELVINATOR, SPEED QUEEN, SORREL, BASSETT and BROYHILL, to drop a few names. The prices were right for us to take possession of a KELVINATOR refrigerator for $299 (reg. $550) and a SPEED QUEEN washer for $269 (reg. $490). Lots of repos plus a good selection of low priced furniture. CK, MC, SC, STAR FINANCING

**
STAR WAREHOUSE OUTLET
2821 Laura Koppe
Houston
Tel. 691-1122
M-S 9-6

AQUARIUMS

Jaws for the heck of it, dive into Aquarama. You're bound to smell something fishy when you shop here, but it won't be the prices. A ten gallon tank with pump was $3.99, colored gravel $1.10 and a filter was $4.99. We could sea all the bargains available and we didn't want any of them to swim out of reach. A variety of fish—Sunsets, Zebras, Black Mollies and mixed Swordtails. Salespeople know their pisces and supplies and are more than willing to help fish you out of your aquarium problems. CK, MC, V

**
AQUARAMA
9 Commerce
Baytown
Tel. 422-0367
M-F 11-7/S 10-6
Sun 12-6

ART OBJECTS

"Hey, pal, can I borrow $8 to buy a new canvas?" Now, that's an Artist's Touch! We took a trip to The Artist's Touch, and found a full spectrum of prints, paintings and sculpture at reasonable prices. A sister store to the Artist's Touch Galleries of 2348 Bissonnet (tel. 523-2763), this store not only helped us paint a pretty picture, but left us with enough cash left to look for a house to hang it in. CK, AE, MC, SC, V

****
THE ARTIST'S TOUCH
738 Westwood Mall
Houston
Tel. 777-8472
M-S 10-9

ART OBJECTS

*
CRAFT INDUSTRIES
78 Woodlake Square
Houston
Tel. 789-8170
M-S 10-5:30/Th 10-9

We could have rubbed our noses in it when we saw the most fabulous collection of Eskimo art south of the north pole. Some pretty crafty soapstone carvings $50-$750 and Eskimo baskets from $30-$50. If the artistic crowd has been giving you the cold shoulder, try improving yourself. They offer courses in ceramics and Ukranian egg painting (red's their favorite color). CK, MC, SC, V

**
**YOUR GRAPHICS
ARE SHOWING**
6100 Westheimer
Houston
Tel. 780-1835
M 12-6/T-W, F-S 10-6
Th 10-8

Are your walls standing around barefaced? If so, drop into Your Graphics Are Showing and learn how to cover them up. Signed, limited editions could be bought for $25-$300, framed and matted. They had lots of etchings, silkscreens, lithos and reproductions hanging around just waiting to decorate home or office. CK, MC, V

AUTO SUPPLIES

**
**HIGHLANDS
DISCOUNT AUTO
SUPPLY**
212 S. Main
Highlands
Tel. 426-5114
M-F 8-6/S 8-5

My heart is in the Highlands but my car is jacked up in the garage. We auto stopped here sooner. Most popular brand names of car parts and equipment for all makes and models were carried at Highlands Discount Auto Supply. If you know how to keep your own car in tune, you'll like their big savings song. No refunds on merchandise that has been installed, but defective merchandise will be replaced with receipt. CK

BABY THINGS

We don't know how many folks diaper year while waiting for a bargain here, but it could be quite a few. The savings at Baby Bargain Ctr. weren't grown up by any means. Prices were cranky (pretty much straight retail). They carried LULLABY, WELSH, STORECRAFT and SIMMONS but they couldn't lull us into buying much at the prices we saw. They offered a warehouse sale the last Sunday of the month, but that didn't pacify us much. CK, MC, V

* .
BABY BARGAIN CTR.
2025 S. Shepherd
Houston
Tel. 526-7033
M-S 9-5:30

BED AND BATH

See write-up under "Buying Services." (New Listings Section)

****
HOUSTON
CONSUMER CENTER

For your Southern Nights or your Afternoon Delights—your bed will never be bored with the likes of ANNE KLEIN, YVES ST. LAURENT, BILL BLASS, OLEG CASSINI at savings of 30-60%. Sleep tight, the prices won't bite. COUNTESS YORK and quilted outline Indian line DAKOTAH (the same designs that retail for a nightmarish $150-$250 elsewhere) are here for $59.97-$119.97. Draperies, sheets, shams, dust ruffles by name designers give you that coordinated look upstairs and downstairs. Towels by FIELDCREST, MARTEX, STEVENS are a soft deal. Tucked away behind Loehmann's, Southern Mills Outlet features over 6000 sq. ft. of first quality bedspreads, comforters, etc. Some irregulars in towels and sheets, but nothing to lose sleep over. Also, 6333 Gulf Freeway, 921-6196. CK, MC, V

****
SOUTHERN MILLS
OUTLET
7425 Southwest Frwy.
Houston
Tel. 988-7499
M-S 9:30-6

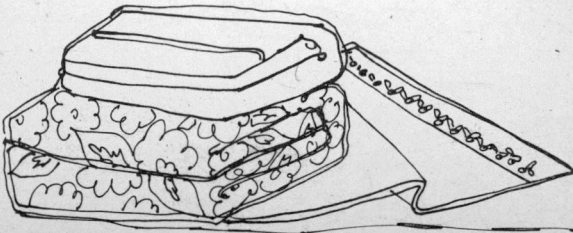

TURN YOUR MATTRESS
BEFORE YOUR MATTRESS TURNS ON YOU

To get the most from your mattress in terms of wear and comfort (and to avoid the effect of sleeping in a hole), turn the mattress over and rotate the head and foot after the first week. Repeat this procedure every two months. A sure cure for lumpy mattress syndrome—and insomnia.

SAVE ME THE WARM SPOT

In shopping for a mattress, ask the salesperson about the Federal Flammability Standard and how their product meets, or—hopefully—exceeds that standard. Even if you don't smoke in bed, and we hope you don't, this is a good thing to know. If the salesperson waffles or gives you a blank look, best buy elsewhere.

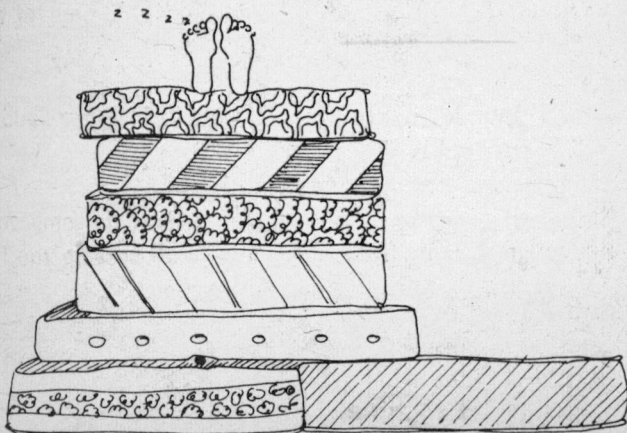

BEST BEDS

A mattress is more than a sack of springs and stuffing. When shopping for your next bed, ask what's inside. Sales personnel will usually show you a cutaway model that has the springs, felt, padding and ticking in neat layers. What you want to know is:

How many steel coils in the base?
(480 is a good number for a king-size.)

How are the springs tied to each other?
(The links should be steel, too.)

Are the springs covered so the insulation won't fall down inside them or bunch up?

Are the edges of the mattress reinforced?

How much of the padding is felt, how much is polyurethane foam? How is it attached to the rest of the structure?

Do the components of the mattress meet the Federal standards of fire safety?

Remember: expensive damask coverings can hide some very sleazy "guts." Don't buy a killer mattress just because you fell in love with the cabbage roses on the covering.

**

THE THREE
WEAVERS SECOND
SHOP
1206 Brooks St.
Houston
Tel. 224-3165
M-F 9:30-4

A trio of drunk drivers? No, The Three Weavers Second Shop was a place to find bargains. We were itching to buy some blankets and afghans at 35% off and the shawls we saw for $22 had us wrapped up. Some famous places we know of carried these same items but at 1/3 more. CK

BEDDING AND MATTRESSES

**

C & E FURNITURE
1111 Conrad Saver
Houston
Tel. 932-7325
M-S 10-8

We didn't see an "E" at C & E, but we did see a sea of bargains. C & E Furniture, alias C & E Model Home Surplus, had undergone a name change but the prices appear to have remained the same. Some of their items, including KING KOIL mattresses could be ordered through catalogs. Lots of big name labels—SINGER, BASSETT, JACK PEARCE CO., PURSE & CO. and LARK— were represented here, but we can't swear to the discount (in the 30-50% range). We saw coffee tables, chairs, sofas and loveseats. CK, MC, V

*

DISCOUNT
MATTRESS AND
FURNITURE
8217 Long Point
Houston
Tel. 932-9937
M-F 9-9/S 9-6

We hate to say it, but Discount Mattress and Furniture didn't make our hearts pound or our wallets open with what they had to offer. You might bed down a bargain on a mattress by SEALY, ENGLANDER, KING KOIL or SERTA but that's about all. We did see a pit sofa (that wasn't the pits) for $899 (reg. $1100). CK, MC, V

*

MODEL HOME
SUPPLY
1727 Campbell Road
Houston
Tel. 468-6420
M-F 8-9/S 8-6/Sun 11-6

The BASSETT we found here was no dog, and we found some SUPREMES, but no Diana Ross. Lots of mattresses on display but very little else. Most of their business is done by catalog, with a $10 delivery charge tacked on for good luck. Salespeople knew their beds. CK, MC, SC, V

Got a complaint, but want to tell someone other than your mother? Try crying on Mr. Kramer's shoulder. Send complaints to: Albert H. Kramer, Director, Bureau of Consumer Products, Federal Trade Commission, Washington, D. C. 20850. Tel. (202) 523-3727.

This store had an ideal location (right across the street from Planned Parenthood). If your planning fails, they figure you're bound to need at least one extra bed! All mattresses manufactured by SUPREME MATTRESS CO., with a full size extra firm and boxspring for $98, and a Queen for $139. Had some dinettes in the $69-$349 price range and a velveteen rocker for $129. Try to find a friend with a truck, since they don't deliver. CK, MC, V

**
MODERN FURNITURE RENTALS, INC.
3536 Fannin
Houston
Tel. 523-0282
M-S 9-5:30

Sleep air what we're after. Call to make sure she's not out to lunch before you go by. Lots of mattresses to bed down on, every size and circumference to curl up on. Saw a king sized set for $399.95, and a twin set for $199.95. $10 delivery fee for mattresses. CK, MC, SC, V

**
SLEEP-AIRE MATTRESS CO.
9251 Gulf Frwy.
Houston
Tel. 941-1845
T-S 10-6/M, Th 10-8:45

BEAUTY SUPPLY

Your Gessner's as good as mine why anyone would shop elsewhere. They had what we wanted at prices we could afford. Unfortunately, we had to buy a bunch to save real money. Licensed beauticians who buy beauty by the bunch get a good deal, but average buyers better think in terms of quantity when shopping here. A good deal was FERMODYL shampoo for $9.95 per quart. A lot of products you wouldn't find at the neighborhood drug store, such as exotic henna rinses. If to curl or not to curl is the question, then Gessner Beauty Supply just might have the answer. CK, MC, V

**
GESSNER BEAUTY SUPPLY
2547 Gessner
Houston
Tel. 462-5511
M-F 9-6/S 9-5

BICYCLES

See write-up under "Buying Services." (New Listings Section)

****
HOUSTON CONSUMER CENTER

77

***
RECYCLED CYCLES
7921 Westheimer
Houston
Tel. 977-1393
M-T, Th-S 10-7
W, Sun 2-7

We hated those gas lines so we dropped by Recycled Cycles and started pumping our legs instead of premium. Mostly trade-ins, priced from $60-$1200. Some children bikes for $39. Did repairs from their own private parts collection. CK

BOATS

***
LYNN SAILBOATS
7717 Gulf Frwy.
Houston
Tel. 644-8161
M-F 9:30-8/S 9-5
Sun 11-4

Here's the poop, Dick. It was easy to stay afloat at Lynn Sailboats. This store tried very hard to stay 10% above cost and kept their overhead below deck by operating on a no frills basis. All prices we were quoted were with trailer, and a CORTEZ at $4600 had us smelling the sea air. Some models were handmade. CK

BOOKS

*
BOOKS 'N' STUFF
1836 Wirt Road
Houston
Tel. 688-7992
M-S 10-7

Books 'N' Stuff had more books than stuff. We toted in a box of old paperbacks and were given a credit of 2 for 1. With approximately 40,000 volumes in the store, selection wasn't our biggest problem. Too bad we're a slow reader. $

*
HUMBLE BOOK DEN
310 Main St.
Humble
Tel. 446-9946
M 11-3/T, Th-F 10-5
S 10-4

Oil we found at Humble was books. It was ever so humble, but it still wasn't home. Paperbacks for .15, but many of these were ripped or torn apart. Had two large rooms filled with books—greater part was of a romantic nature. Non-fiction and hobby books also available. All books were second-hand, but a lot of the prices were first rate. $

**
KENDRICK BOOK STORE
2429 Rice Blvd.
Houston
Tel. 528-3388
M-F 9:30-5:30/S 9-5

By hook or crook, you're bound to find a book. Some popular novels and lots of reference books to refer to. They're been there 19 years and take their business very seriously. We spied some hard to find, out of print books. If you're on the look for that certain book, check every nook. CK, MC

BOOTS

Everybody would want to die with their boots on if they came from Boot Center Co. Custom made boots, for the hard to fit foot, started at $50. RED WING and IRISH SETTER work boots fit any job at $20 less than retail. We didn't stick our heads in the sand when we saw Ostrich boots for $225 (reg. $375). Men's LEVIS at $13 were a pleasant surprise. CK, MC, V

***
BOOT CENTER CO.
702 Center
Deer Park
Tel. 479-7891
M-F 9-6/S 9-5

The names were the same (ACME, DURANGO) but the prices were enough to convict even the smartest shoppers. We couldn't rustle up too many bargains since most of their boots grazed the $35-$70 range. The personnel didn't sweep us off our feet and the savings (?) didn't have much sole. $

*
BOOT LAND
1006 N. Shepherd
Houston
No phone listed
M-S 9:15-6:30

This country boy just may become a city slicker. With such names as ACME, NOCONA, TONY LAMA, JUSTIN and prices to match, he could make anybody's social register. All the bargains end in .88, and there were plenty of 'em. Take a tour of the back room to see the specials, and even the kids can get in on this round up. CK, MC, V

**
COUNTRY BOY
BOOTS
120 Tatar
Pasadena
Tel. 473-9105
M-S 9-7

We stepped in it and didn't mind a bit. Checked out the bargains in this corral and roped us some shark skin boots for $59. The water buffalo weren't all wet at $44. About 70% of the merchandise was factory irregulars, with the rest being first quality. They manufacture their own boots under the brand, COWTOWN. CK, MC

***
COWTOWN BOOT
FACTORY OUTLET
5568 N. Freeway
Houston
Tel. 694-2150
M-S 10-6/F 10-9

Found some pretty good looking stock in this barn. Dress boots started at $49.88 and the $16 ones were made for working. JUSTIN lizard boots reared their heads at $145, and the TONY LAMA elephant boots at $150 were worth remembering. This store was a treat to the feet. CK, MC, V

**
JOHN'S BOOT BARN
109 E. Highway 90
Dayton
Tel. 258-7877
M-S 8-6

Just because we thought they were so good looking, just because we thought they were so much fun, we decided to buy up some of the DINGO, DURANGO and ACME boots. Women's sizes 3-10; men's 6½-15. The TONY LAMA'S started at $40 and the jeans (LEVIS, WRANGLERS) finished off at $9.88-$14.95. CK, MC, SC, V

*
JUST BOOTS
12310 Hempstead Hwy.
Houston
Tel. 462-8293
M-S 9-7

BOOTS

*

**KICKER WESTERN
STORE**
11204 Hempstead Hwy.
Tel. 686-6547
M-S 10-6

We took a shower and shaved with our Schick, Kicker, then dropped by your neat store. We got our kicks from champagne and Kicker Western Store. Starting price for better boots were $39. Lots of bubbly labels—TONY LAMA, NOCONA, TEXAS and DINGO. Twenty different styles for the guys and ten for the gals. Keep this under your cowboy hat—jeans were retail. CK, AE, DC, MC, SC, V

**

**SHOE WORLD AND
WESTERN WEAR**
820 Main
Liberty
Tel. 336-6791
M-F 8-7/S 8-8

We bet our boots you'll like Shoe World and Western World. TONY LAMA, ACME, JUSTIN and DINGO boots were all corralled here. Carried DEE CEE western shirts and WRANGLERS to go with 'em. The 20% savings made us put another bargain notch in our belts (they had those too). We could have shoed any size critter (shoes start at 0; boots at size 4). CK, MC, V

BRIDAL

***

**BRIDAL
ASSORTMENTS, INC.**
3140 North St.
Beaumont
Tel. 892-0352
M-S 9:30-5/T 9:30-8

Mickey Rooney had a Bridal Assortment, for sure. Whether its your first plunge (miss) or your tenth (mess), you will love the savings at this Bridal Assortments. Full run of sizes in most styles—not just a sample shop. Labels like VICKY VAUGHAN, DATE MAKER, SYLVIA ANN, MALIA and MR. WALTER were perfect attendants for any wedding. With savings on some items up to 50%, you could save a mint for the honeymoon. CK, MC, V

*

BRIDAL BOUTIQUE
2350 Calder
Beaumont
Tel. 833-2091
M-S 9:30-5:30
T 9:30-8:30

Here comes the bride, slippin' in wearing a NADINE, ALFRED WEBER or SYLVIA ANN. With color, design, lots of fashion or fad, this little boutique is unique. Most of the store was regular price but they carried sales frequently in their mark-down room in the front of the store. Formals priced from $45-$200. It was easy to promise to shop there till death we did part. CK, MC, V

80

We left Shirley's singing, "Get me to the church on time." At the end of the season, samples are sold at ½ price and the designer originals made us start thinking of honeymoon in June. Prices on originals were full price, but their frequent sales could help you catch a bouquet of savings. CK, MC, V

*
BRIDES BY SHIRLEY
2200 Main
Houston
Tel. 659-8787
T-W, F 10-6
M, Th 10-8:30
S 9:30-5:30

CAMERAS

This store clicked with us. We shutter to think of the high prices we saw elsewhere. They offered courses for $35 on print, composition and developing. We snapped up a CANON for $169 (reg. $263). NIKON, PENTAX, MINOLTA, KONICA and CHINON were all posed prettily and cheaply on their shelves. We could hardly wait to see what other bargains they were going to develop. Visit other locations at 12120 Gulf Freeway and I-45 at North Belt. CK, MC, AE, SC, V

***
TOTAL CAMERA
6128 Westheimer
Houston
Tel. 784-2889
M-F 9:30-9/S 9:30-6

CANDLES

Not only would Jack have to be nimble at FAROY CANDLES, but he'd have to be a super sleuth to find out what's downstairs. They won't tell you on the phone. We dropped by and found butterfly shaped floating candles and plenty of perfume and wax to make our own designer originals. Most everything was 20-50% off and looked (nearly) as good as new. Snuff said. CK

***
FAROY CANDLES
SECOND SHOP
7915 Westglen
Houston
Tel. 781-1616
M-F 9-3:30

Hop in your Van and Horn in on a good deal. They may handle seconds, but this store was first rate. Offered 50% savings on painted wood and plexiglas candle holders, frames, and decorative accessories. The stock changes constantly and ranges in size from one candle holder to six tiers. Cheerful and knowledgeable clerks really lighted up our day. CK

***
VAN HORN AND
HAYWARD SECONDS
SHOP
6115 Skyline
Houston
Tel. 782-8532
M-Th 9:30-4

****
WICKS 'N' STICKS
FACTORY OUTLET
6937 Flintlock
Houston
Tel. 466-5876
M-S 8-5

This candle factory gave us scents for cents. The aromas of magnolia, musk, strawberry and pina colada scent our noses into a frenzy. We cast our ballot for the votive candles, which were eight for $1.49. Standard 3" X 6" were two for $2.31 (reg. $4.25). Lots of animal sculpture, mainly dogs. Nothing wick-ed about their salespeople—an absolute delight to chat with. You'd have to burn the candle at both ends to get around to all the bargains in this store, but it could be worth the effort. CK, MC, SC, V

CARPET AND FLOOR COVERINGS

**
THE ALAN STORE
9319 Stella Link
Houston
Tel. 666-1821
M-S 9:30-5:30

Swatch it, Alan! You're upsetting the competition. None of these carpets were able to fly, but the prices were enough to make us soar (not sore) on our own power. Extremely friendly people who didn't sweep anything under the rug. Saw some tapestry fabric for $10.99/yd. (reg. $25) and some 54" COHAMA for $5.25 (reg. $12). The best deals were on carpet remnants in the back of the store. CK, MC, V

**
DISCOUNT CARPET
& SALVAGE CENTER
1140 Railroad
Beaumont
Tel. 838-0366
M-F 8:30-5:30

A fuzzy thing happened on the way to the carpetorium. We got tickled at the great savings we found on SALEM, LUDLOW, SPACEWAY and HORIZON carpet. Prices start at $3.99/sq. yd. and spiral upwards from there. Back of store had all types of salvage from lumber to painting supplies. If you don't sweep up any of the terrific carpet buys, stroll over to the linoleum and vinyl floor coverings. Good deals there, too. All sales final; no returns. CK, MC, V

*
DISCOUNT TILE
MART
8304 Long Point
Houston
Tel. 932-1446
M-F 9:30-6/S 9:30-5

If you're oriented toward a new look for your floor, this store just might have what you need. Good prices on Italian, Japanese, mosaic and ARMSTRONG vinyl tile. Marble tiles were $3/sq. ft. Will do installation but the price varies with the size of the tile. CK

See write-up under "Buying Services." (New Listings Section)

****
HOUSTON
CONSUMER CENTER

Mr. Carpet had most places beat with rug prices that didn't just lie around. Indoor-outdoor carpet $4.99/yd., with four experts to lay it all at your feet. One day installation service. Savings of 40% plus were noted and the selection of carpeting ranged from moderate to plush in quality. Check directory for other locations. CK, V

**
MR. CARPET
8213 Long Point
Houston
Tel. 932-1100
M-F 9-8/S 9-7

We racked up some real bargains at Remnant Rack. With BIGELOW, CONGOLEUM, SOLARIUM, VENTURE and TREND available, every price we saw was an easy shot to the pocket. Savings of 50% on carpeting and vinyl. Charges will add 5% to your bill, but at those prices we were calling the shots. CK, MC, V

**
REMNANT RACK
2514 Suffolk
Houston
No phone listed
M-S 8-5

We'll take it, but someone else will have to lay it. (Last time I laid carpet, we lost a roller skate, two books and our poodle). The buys on SOLARIUM and CONGOLEUM flooring made us start looking for a "How-To Book" so we could take advantage of the savings. We found formica at about 1/2 price, which was nice. The big deals are in the back room—remnants and discounted patterns. CK

**
TAKE IT AND LAY IT
FLOOR CORRAL
2504 Bissonnet
Houston
No phone listed
M-F 7-5/Th 7-9

CAR RENTAL

We found it to be as thrilling as a 50-mile ride in a Sherman tank—Rent A Heap—Cheap. Cars ranged from 1965-75 models with a few existing dents, but the prices didn't put a dent in our wallet. Daily $9.50 and weekly $55 rates with 50 miles free per day and 350 per week took us for a ride. Pick up trucks were rented for $9.50-$12.50 daily, depending on what we needed to haul. If you need to travel, but don't want the hassle of ownership, this could be the answer to your problems. CK, AE, CB, MC, V

RENT A HEAP—
CHEAP
5857 Westheimer
Houston
Tel. 977-7771
M-F 8:30-5:30
S 8:30-12

RENT-A-RELIC, INC.
6869 Telephone Road
Houston
Tel. 641-6671
M-F 8:30-5:30

If you long for the good ole days and you used to be dirt poor, then Rent-A-Relic, Inc. will do their best to get you back to the past. Most of the cars were relics (1971-73) and the older the car, the cheaper it was to rent. Rates were $9 a day/plus .10 a mile to $11 a day/plus .10 a mile. Their weekly rates went from $55 to $70 a week. After riding in these vintage, mid-sized cars, the future looks brighter and brighter. CK, MC, DC, AE, V

CARS AND TRUCKS

NR
UNITED STATES
POSTAL SERVICE
7511 N. Shepherd
Houston
Tel. 226-5275
(for information)
Periodic; M-F 9-4:30

We'd have bought one of their cute little jeeps, but rumor had it that no matter where you wanted to go, it would take you twice the usual time to get there. Prices range from $700-$1250 for 1971-72 models. Sales are held 2-3 times per year with 120 vehicles per auction. With the price of postage, we never dreamed the postal service needed the extra cash! CK

CATALOG SHOWROOMS

Catalog showrooms are not technically "outlets", but some of the biggies carry name brand merchandise—and stuff you never heard of—at USUALLY less than retail. The idea in our minds behind the catalog showrooms is to lure you into the store with a glossy 4-color "wish book", let you browse until you find something you can't resist (the rubber raft, the cut-out bra, the porcelain toothbrush holder), and then get you to fill out an order form. Do Not Fold, Staple or Pass Go, but go directly to the ordering desk. The showroom elves will locate the electric peanut butter maker, process the order, push a conveyor belt button and deliver it to the central check-out stand. Not much faster than waiting for your seeds to arrive from Wisconsin, though you won't have to take a lot of guff from the mailman. Some showrooms specialize; others handle a little bit of everything. Here's a sampling of catalog showrooms in Houston:

UNITED JEWELERS AND DISTRIBUTORS
5819 Gulf Freeway
Tel. 926-9411
M, Th-F 10-9/T-W, S 10-6

4405 Main
Tel. 526-6326
M, Th 10-9/T-S 10-6

11150 North Freeway
Tel. 448-7311

2301 S. Voss Road
Tel. 783-0270
M-F 10-9/S 10-6

900 W. Texas Avenue
Baytown
Tel. (713) 427-6641
M-F 10-9/S 10-6

610 Memorial City Shop. Ctr.
Tel. 464-4938
M-S 10-9

GENERAL WHOLESALE PRODUCTS
General Wholesale Building
1398 Harris Street
Tel. 672-1666

W. BELL AND COMPANY
1200 Main
Tel. 658-8701
M-S 9:30-5:30

WILSON'S JEWELERS AND DISTRIBUTORS
144 Gulfgate Mall
Tel. 641-5071
M-S 10-9 (all stores)

10225 Katy Freeway
Tel. 461-3388

6900 Southwest Freeway
Tel. 783-8820

5319 FM 1960 West
Tel. 440-9111

CHILDREN'S WEAR

Smart, Mart! Kid's clothing for less. The Apparel Mart was a little short on junior apparel (they didn't have any) but we did find some comfort in sleepwear at 40% off. Factory direct shopping in robes, pajamas, gowns and lacy children's stuff. Actually, the selection made us a bit tired, so we grabbed some sleepers and ran on home to bed. Also in Bay City, Columbus (take a chance), Rosenburg, El Campo (drive down in el camper), Alvin and Port Lavaca. CK

***
THE APPAREL MART
2615 Avenue H
Rosenberg
Tel. 232-3676
M-S 9-5:30

For every little haute 'n' tot. The Children's Gingerbread House offered this and more. Name brands such as THEE & ME, NAN-NATTE, FANTASIA, LITTLE WORLD and KATE GREENAWAY are sugar-coated at 1/3 off. Large monogram business on everything from underpants to barrettes. Their yard tent sales are held periodically under the canopy with savings and gingerbread served in quantity. CK, AE, DC, MC, V

****
CHILDREN'S GINGERBREAD HOUSE
1635 Blalock Road
Houston
Tel. 467-2141
M-S 10-6

85

**
KID'S KLOTHES
KLOSET
14625½ Memorial
Houston
Tel. 497-5899
M-S 10-5

This Kid's Klothes Kloset was no mess! Filled to the brim with closeouts, samples, irregulars and discontinued items at the approximate 20% off range. Brands such as JUST GIRLS, LEMON DROPS, PUMPLIN, YOUNG LAND, CINDERELLA, LEVI and BILLY THE KID were popping up everywhere. For the young set, this store made a great hide out. CK, MC, V

COSTUMES

NR
SOUTHERN
IMPORTERS
4825 San Jacinto
Houston
Tel. 524-8236
M-S 8:30-5:30

They had horse masks (front half) plus loads more. Birds nest, hula shirts, shells, spot lights and costumes were the customary offerings at this store. It was hard to compare prices since not many stores carried piggie faces as standard shelve items. Largest selection was in masks, priced from $16-$80. CK, MC, V

A TREATISE ON COUPONS AND REFUNDING

YIPPEE, CLIPPEE!

There are numerous bulletins printed monthly which usually list at least 100 new refund offers each issue. Cost of the bulletins range from $6-$9 per year. Most refunds are available to anyone having knowledge of the offer and a refund form. Refund bulletins provide all the details of a refund, often indicate whether an official refund form is necessary to get the refund, contain ads by people wanting to exchange refund forms and cash-off coupons and include information concerning which companies will send forms to you upon request.

A very part-time refunder we know figures she received $300-$400 per year in refunds which does not include coupons for free products and free "premiums" (gift items such as T-shirts, electric outlet timer, small tool kit, utensils, etc.). Because of all of the buy one, two, or three and get one free offers, she has not bought ketchup, salad dressings, facial tissue or cake mixes in years!

For a list of publications and subscription information, you can send a large self-addressed, stamped envelope to:

Bunch of Editors (this is an organization of bulletin editors)
7626 22nd Street
Sacramento, California 95832

MANUFACTURERS' COUPON EXCHANGES

AMERICAN COUPON TRADE SERVICE, P.O. Box 26047, Oklahoma City, Oklahoma 73126, $10 for 6 mo., $15 yr. subscription. Up to $50 worth of coupons can be exchanged for the brand coupons you desire on a basis of a $1 worth of coupons for every $2 worth sent. This company's motto is, "Coupons and people can be redeemed by their maker."

JEEPERS CREEPERS REFUND PEEPERS, Box 1258, Thousand Oaks, California 91360. Learn to cut coupons and save on nationally advertised brands. For $6.75 a year, you can join this coupon-cutting and swapping service.

SANSONE'S COUPON EXCHANGE CLUB, 1592 North A1A, Satellite Beach, Florida 32937, $3 membership for a year, .75 handling charge for every $5 block of coupons sent with no less than sixty days to expiration. Subscriber provides club with a list of desired coupons.

CRAFTS AND HOBBY SUPPLIES

We've never been spastic over plastic, but this store gave us a clear view of the goods. Acrylics in a variety of sizes. Opaque, smoked and clear acrylic cut-offs for the see through price of $1.90 per sq. ft., for the 1/16" thickness. CK

*
A-1 PLASTICS
5822 Southwest Frwy.
Houston
Tel. 785-3040
M-F 8-5/S 8-1

You may apply for the 20% discount offered here if you're the sort who is missing an ear or enjoys painting chapel ceilings on your back (full time). Students get the cut rates too, but we discovered what they mean by "starving artist". Who could afford to eat after giving $11.25-$200 for Eberhardt-Faber easels? Grandma Moses would have gone off her rocker. CK, MC, V

*
ART SUPPLY
915 Richmond Ave.
Houston
Tel. 526-2691
M-F 9-6/S 9-4

This store didn't string us along. We found a bead for every need. No beady-eyed sales people, either. Always a great source for pastel wooden beads. Their prices were well strung, from .18 for brass to .65 for 14K gold. Grab some string and go after these unbeadable prices. CK, MC, V

****
THE BEAD SHOP
2476 Times Blvd.
Houston
Tel. 523-9350
M-S 10:30-6

*
CADILLAC PLASTICS
5031 Gulf Frwy.
Houston
Tel. 928-2581
M-F 8:30-5/S 9-12

A solid, plastic Cadillac? The car of the future, no doubt, as the autos shrink and the prices go up. Well, if you every need a pound of plastic but don't have a buck, cheer up. Cadillac Plastics sold it to us for .75. They cut plastic right on the spot and we could see through their work. They will fit all your plastic needs to a tee! CK

**
ART LAND, INC.
6651 N. Gessner
Houston
Tel. 462-3363
M, Th 9:30-9/S 9:30-5
T, W, F 9:30-6

A good art supply store (Discount Art Supplies) by any other name (Art Land, Inc.) was a great art store! They were stocking LANGNICKEL brushes because quality was similar to GRUMBACHER (at 1/3 the price). Lots of stock, including brushes, sketch books and paints of course. Buyers beware, 'cause they might try to frame you in their large custom framing department. We just might take the rap, since the selection of odd size frames was worth doing time for. CK, AE, MC, V

****
MICHAEL'S
I-59/FM 1960
Bender Square S.C.
Humble
Tel. 446-0211
M-S 10-9/Sun 12-6

My culls at Michael's were still better than I had found at most frame stores. Over 10,000 different frames available. They did all their framing on the spot with an 8-30 minute wait. Stocked lots of other goodies for keeping idle hands busy, such as needle craft and flower making kits. Store personnel was willing to lend a helping hand to rookie craftsmen. All we had to do was ask. CK, MC, V

**
**PICK A FRAME
CUSTOM FRAMING
AND GALLERY**
9809 Harwin
Houston
Tel. 977-1245
M-Th 10-6/F 10-1
S 10-3

"Pick a Frame" is not a new game show for crooks who wish to blame others for their crimes. It is a place where we picked our favorite frame from a selection that ran from ornate wood to black metal. Frames were discounted 15% if they did the work, and 35% if we did it. Frames started at $20 with glass and dry mounting extra. Also had unframed sofa-sized pictures from $15-$45. Well organized and friendly. CK, MC, V

Outstanding bargains are Reginia's claim to frame and fortune. We found a stock of 30,000, pre-made and ready to go in all shapes, sizes and colors. Big three paints: WINDSOR NEWTON, PERMANENT PIGMENT and PERMELBA at 30% off list. FREDERICKS & WOLSEY canvases, $2.57 for a 16 X 20; others as low as $1.98 for the 14 X 18 size. Self-service and no air-conditioning, but worth it for the savings. CK

****
REGINIA'S WHOLE-SALE FRAMES
7100 No. Loop East
Houston
Tel. 672-2871
M-F 9-5/S 9-2

This was one gem of a store. Vogel's had everything for the do-it-yourself jeweler, including clasps, beads, glue and wire-cutters. Also had finished jewelry, such as 14K 18" "S" chain for $16.50, coral branch necklace on string for $11.50 and black mother of pearl for $4.50. These bargains had us strung out over which one to buy first. CK

***
VOGEL'S
4310 W.T.C. Jester Blvd
Houston
Tel. 681-9601
M-F 8:30-5

CURIOS

A little bit of Mexico without crossing the border. Lots of touristy goodies for tourist prices. Many plaster statues and wrought iron light fixtures. Cheap pinatas, too. If you hear Mexico calling (collect) and you can't afford to answer, drop by Spanish Imports. CK

*
SPANISH IMPORTS
3315-17 Washington
Houston
No phone listed
M-S 9:30-5:30

CUSTOM CLOTHING

**

**KAUWMI HAPPY
DRESSES**
4406 Breakwood
Houston
Tel. 723-4568
By appt. only

Kauwmi, my melancholy baby, will perk
you up in a hurry! Kauwmi may have
moved, but her fashions were still in the
same place—number one! Sculpting her fabrics to fit your figure made for a perfect
fit. A batik or cotton wrap around skirt in
the one-of-a-kind variety covered us up
beautifully for $58-$78. Call for an appointment since she works from her home. You'll
be happy and look snappy in KAUWMI
Happy Dresses. CK

DEPARTMENT STORE WAREHOUSES

**

**FOLEY'S
WAREHOUSE**
4500 Gulf Frwy.
Houston
Tel. 651-6416
M-S 10-9

A warehouse that offers furniture, carpet,
some major appliances and T.V.'s, floor
samples, discontinued items, and some regular items at discount prices. Mind your bargain hunting P's and Q's and maybe you'll
find a thrill of a deal. CK

**

J.C. PENNEY
1501 Seamist
Houston
Tel. 684-7515
S 9-5

Even J. C. counts his pennies. Saturday
sales on damaged furniture, appliances and
T.V.'s. CK, PENNEY'S CHARGE

**

**MONTGOMERY
WARD WAREHOUSE**
2720 Clinton
Houston
Tel. 932-2483
M-S 8:30-5

Since Ward's employees shopped here, there
must be some bargains. Outlet for damaged
furniture, appliances, T.V.'s and some
returned merchandise. CK, WARD'S
CHARGE

**

**OSHMAN'S
WAREHOUSE**
2223 S. Wayside
Houston
Tel. 928-5789
M, W, F 10-9
T, Th, S 10-6

Twenty Oshman stores in Houston send all
extra merchandise to this warehouse at the
end of each sporting season. This place had
much on the ball (foot, basket, base, tennis,
soccer, golf). If you're game enough, you
could hit a hole in one. CK, MC, V

Short for "Give It To Our Faithful Friends". This was a little misleading. They weren't giving anything away, no matter how faithful we were. The discounted prices on regular Sakowitz merchandise was worth a peek, so we took a quick look. The selection at the end of the season could be great, but like all of Texas, it occasionally suffers from dry spells. DC, AE, SAKOWITZ CHARGE

**
SAKOWITZ
G.I.T.O.F.F.
Gulf Gate S.C.
Houston
Tel. 641-6444
M, Th-F 10-9/S 10-6
T-W 10-5:30

This has to be where the real America shops! Small appliances, T.V.'s, lamps, furniture and clothing from their catalog store in Dallas, with some merchandise from Houston. If you love to see your furniture in everyone else's house, do rush down. CK, SEARS CHARGE

*
SEARS ROEBUCK
CATALOG SURPLUS
STORE
11520 Gulf Frwy.
Houston
Tel. 944-8410
M-F 9:30-9/S 9:30-6

If you can't afford steak, try Weiner's. Plenty to choose from amidst the traditional discount atmosphere. Orderly, clean and easy to shop in. Many major brands such as LEVI's were not discounted, but they were marked down occasionally. Carried shoes for the whole family. Take a look for yourself and you just may end up saying, "Hot Dog"! CK, MC, V

**
WEINER'S DEPART-
MENT STORE
4037 Westheimer
Houston
Tel. 622-4210
M-S 9-9

DINETTES, DINING ROOMS

You're a prince, Phillip. How about a 30" X 40" butcher block table for $130? This warehouse outlet offered buys on STONE-VILLE, BASSETT and DAYSTROM. Savings of 20-40% let us put more meat on an attractive dining table. CK, MC, SC, V

**
PHILLIPS DISCOUNT
DINETTES
9805-L Harwin Dr.
Houston
Tel. 977-7844
M; Th 10-8/T-W 10-6
S 10-5:30

DOLL HOUSES

NR
LITTLE FOLKS
ORIGINALS
1015B E. Harris
Pasadena
Tel. 473-4882
T-S 9-5

If you're looking for the teentsy prices we talked about last year, forget it. Doll houses once were a bargain at $39.95—Mr. Guest, our host, reported that everyone who walked in went for the higher priced spreads, so they've phased out the "cheapies". (He should try to remember what that philosophy did to the Chrysler Corp.) Each doll house is built to client's specifications and prices now begin at $150. Plan on eight weeks' wait. They are exquisite, with their custom wallpapers, paint, fixtures and carpeting. Extras ARE extra: $30 for a ROPER gas range, $5 for a 5-piece dinette set and anywhere from $8-$100 for a brass bed. CK

DRAPERIES AND WINDOW TREATMENTS

****
HOUSTON
CONSUMER CENTER

See write-up under "Buying Services." (New Listings Section)

***
WINDOW FASHIONS,
ETC.
9521-F Westheimer
Houston
Tel. 780-9521
M-F 10-5:30/Th 10-8
S 10-3

Our verdict is that this is an open and shut case for great savings on the latest in blinds, shutters and shades. No need to drop a stitch when you realize that LEVELOR, BALI, drape and spread materials go at 30-40% off. Installation included; measurements extra. CK, MC

EYEWEAR

*
FRAME 'N' LENS
41 Woodlake Square
Houston
Tel. 783-8343
M-S 10-6/Th 10-9

All those with a flair for fashion said, "eye," to Frame 'N' Lens. All those with a flair for saving money said, "bye". Frames by OSCAR DE LA RENTA, DIANE VON FURSTENBERG, BILL BLASS, RALPH LAUREN, GEOFFREY BEENE, ANNE KLEIN and PUCCI. CK, MC, V

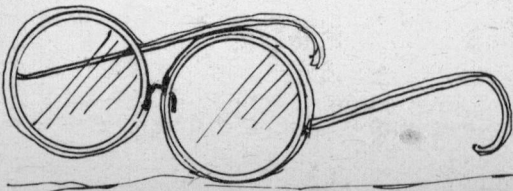

et rid of your old fashioned, boring, square"-framed eyes-cubes. Get with it in he fantastic eyewear from Royal Optical. verything we priced was 50% off, including esigner frames by PIERRE CARDIN, LEG CASSINI, OSCAR DE LA RENTA nd CHRISTIAN DIOR. There is a $10 dis-ensing fee. We found these super bargains t their other locations, too. Brazos Mall in ake Jackson (297-1313), 6710 Marinette 774-4772), 9558 Hempstead (686-7619) nd 2416 University (522-9222). CK, MC, V

****
ROYAL OPTICAL
Baybrook Mall
19400 Gulf Frwy.
Tel. 488-3490
M-S 10-9

FABRIC

he Calico Cat would be purr-fectly delight-d with the abundance of fabrics here. We reened at the (very) slightly flawed mer-handise—all marked ½ off. However, our whiskers curled a bit when we observed hat not all were at true savings, notably he GRABER drapery rods and accessories. Jo need to worry about cutting corners—hey'll make up drapes at $7/panel—lined r not. CK, MC, V

**
CALICO CORNERS
9198 Old Katy Road
Houston
Tel. 464-8653
M-S 10-5:30/Th 10-8

These are a few of our favorite fabric things: WAVERLY, JOHN WOLF, COHAMA, RIV-ERDALE and P. KAUFMAN. 30-40% sav-ngs on most 54" fabrics and bargains galore n bins on the floor. The largest container eld gobs upon oodles of remnants for $1/ ard! CK, MC, AE, V

**
FABRIC AND THINGS
6114 Richmond Ave.
Houston
Tel. 783-3810
M-F 10-6/Th 10-9
S 10-4

$6.95 is the top price on RIVERDALE and BLOOMCRAFT. Why? Because it's all actory-direct. And, since they buy through distributors, WAVERLY, SCHUMACHER nd AMERICAN FABRICS go at $2 off per ard. Cool Haitian cottons are $8.95, HER-CULON from $6.95-$9.95/yd. Three fabric-illed rooms—please don't drool on the goods. CK

***
FACTORY FABRIC OUTLET
7010 Alder
Houston
Tel. 667-2548
M-Th 9:30-4:30
F-S 9:30-12

**

**HOUSTON FABRIC
CENTER**
2712 Capitol
Houston
Tel. 225-9026
M-F 9-6/S 9-4

The place was NOT a mess! It was just a
little unorganized, but at these prices, who
cares? Mill ends were discounted 25-50%
and you could order from their books at
20% off. SCHUMACHER, RIVERDALE
and BLOOMCRAFT did make an appear
ance and they even carried supplies to make
your own bedspreads. Be it bed, window or
floor, this store can cover the subject. CK,
AE, MC, V

****

LEGGETT FABRICS
2702 Capitol
Houston
Tel. 222-2471
M-F 7:30-6/T 7:30-9

If you miss your bus, Leggett! We found it
was the place to go. Many upholsterer
shopped there for their supplies. Most
fabrics were $7/yd. with a large offering of
caning, cording, tacks and padding. DAVID
& DASH, RIVERDALE and SCHUMACH
ER fabrics were all on display and we al
most split our seams taking a look at all the
bargains. CK

***

M & M FABRICS
921 Seabreeze
La Porte
Tel. 471-5542
Call for hours

We can safely say these M & M's won't
melt in your hand or mess up your purse.
Most fabrics were $7-$15 per yd., with rem
nants $3 per yd. More of an upholstery shop
than drapery, we found RONATEX and
JACQUARD to cover up with. Keep
rather irregular hours, so give them a ring-a-
ding before you drop by. CK

****

**MILL OUTLET
FABRICS**
617 Highway 288
Clute South of 10
Tel. 265-7261
M-S 9-6

This store appeared to be a mill end burial
ground, but we snooped around and found
they buy bunches direct from the factory.
Had upholstery fabrics and yard goods by
the mile. Their inventory was a bit over
whelming, but so was the 50% discount they
offered. CK, MC, V

**

**PAULETT'S FABRIC
SHOP**
110 E. Harris
Pasadena
Tel. 472-7167
M 9-8/T-S 9-6

We basted in the sew nice prices at Paulett's
Fabric Shop. Prices appeared to be 20%
less than others in the area, and the big
selection of fabrics, helpful sales personnel
had us zig zagging from bargain to bargain.
CK, MC, V

FAMILY WEAR

(Men's, Women's, Children's)

Don't expect them to bill and coo over you here unless you happen to be a local yokel. A degree from the Wharton School of Business would be of less value than one from Wharton High. NO SHOPLIFTING signs plastered throughout and they wouldn't take our check without a local ID. Non-billable items included VAN HEUSEN shirts for $5 and CALIFORNIA GIRL T-shirts $3-$5. Was that Bill behind those FOSTER GRANTS (at an eye-opening $4)? Second location in Tomball (Tom's Dollar Store?). CK (with ID)

*
BILL'S DOLLAR STORE
W. Milam
Wharton South of 28
Tel. 532-2389
M-S 9-5:30

Local Babel has it that this Tower is the place to go for ACT III and JONATHAN LOGAN sportswear. When we dropped by, the tower was leaning toward a large quantity of name-brand menswear as well: ADIDAS and LA COSTA shirts were cheap, PIERRE CARDIN belts only $3.95 and 100% wool suits an inferno-ly low $54.95. Groceries, fabric, CORNINGWARE weren't worth buttressing your fortresses for. CK, MC, V

***
TOWER BARGAIN CENTER
1320 Avenue F
Bay City S. of 28
Tel. 245-9539
M-S 9-5:30

FARMERS' MARKETS

Lettuce lead you to this roadside market just off 610N. Produce cash only and walk away with a cornucopia of savings on all fruits and vegetables. We saw zucchini at $.49/lb., cantaloupes .40/ea., beans .39/lb. and apples .49/lb. Watermelons were a succulent .10/lb. Hen fruit, an egg-ceptional .79 per dozen. MRS. RENFRO'S pickled chow-chow in the canned goods section, along with pickled eggs at $7.95 for a 5 lb. jar. Cooperative displays made shopping a pleasure. $

NR
FARMER'S CO-OP
2520 Airline Dr.
Houston
Tel. 862-8866
M-Sun 6AM-10 PM

What a friend we have in cheeses! Cheeselovers International is your friend, too, offering unusual and exotic cheese choices to members at a little above wholesale. Small membership fee. Write for information to Box 1200, Westburg, N.Y. 11590.

***
FREDLYN CORP.
9941 Harwin
Houston
Tel. 781-2710
M-F 8:30-5/S 8:30-12

Looks like Fred and Lyn took a hint from Philbert and Hazel. They've squirreled away a stockpile of pecans, cashews, etc., for the Nut Huts around town, but walnut object to selling 'em in quantity if you pine for nuts. The more you buy, the less you shell out—20-30% less than anywhere else. Pistachios (natural or red) $4.95 and $5.45/lb. Cashews were $5.60/lb., pecans $4/lb. and macadamias $8/lb. CK

FIREPLACE EQUIPMENT

**
THE BRASS SHOP
2120 Highway 146
Houston
Tel. 474-2944
T-S 9-6

We entered poker-faced, never expecting to find that prices are logged in at substantial savings. Custom firescreens manufactured on the premises, thus smoking out the middle man. Our bellows expanded over this hot stuff! CK, MC, V, SC, DC

FLEA MARKETS

***
COLE'S FLEA MARKET
1020 N. Main (Hwy. 35)
Pearland
Tel. 485-2277
F-Sun 8:30-5:30

We are reminded of Cole's law: chopped cabbage. A different cole is the one who has a midnight sale the second Friday each month for Cole's Midnight Madness sale. You can shop regular hours also among the 400 dealers gathered under one roof. Fine antiques, tools and plants ignited our urge to acquire. We didn't get raked over the coals on the prices, either! $

*
DOWN TO EARTH FLEA MARKET
1217 Crosstimbers
Houston
No phone listed
Sun-S 9-6

We got Down To Earth here the same way Skylab did. WHAM! No lofty prices—just good bargains. We saw some unusual furniture and glassware. This piece of terra firma, between N. Sheperd and Airline, may have just the item you seek. Chairs at $5 each were a steal. Old Singer sewing machines and many other antiques. Things were looking up at Down To Earth. All sales final. CK

SOME TIPS FROM
THE LAND OF THE FLEA AND THE BRAVE

Flea Market Shopping

1. Always wear old clothes and comfortable shoes to a flea market.

2. Know the prices. If you don't know, ask. Try not to ask, "Is this AMERICAN money?"

3. Browse first, buy later.

4. Carry only as much money as your budget will permit. Leave the checkbook at home. This precaution has been known to save marriages, lives, and psychiatrist bills.

5. ALWAYS ask, "Will you take less for this?" Smile a lot when you say it. The seller may take pity on you.

6. Try not to think of how rich you'd be if Grandma hadn't given everything to Goodwill.

7. When touring with children, locate the "comfort stations" early. Decide how much pocket money the kids will carry, and stick with that amount. Leave them alone to negotiate their own purchases.

8. If you get crazy and buy the stuffed weasel, don't panic. There's always another flea market to unload it on some stuffed weasel lover.

***
**FARMERS' MARKET
TRADING FAIR**
700 Town & Country
Houston
Tel. 467-2506
F-Sun 9-6

Sip a little champagne ($1 for a glass) but don't let the bubbly take control or you're bound to walk out with more than you bargained for—including a headache. You'll want a clear head when shopping to your heart's content. Over 140 shops filled with plants, antiques, jewelry and other collectibles. $

****
**FOUR SEASONS
COMMON MKT., INC.**
4412 N. Shepherd
Houston
Tel. 697-4765
M, Th, F 10-6
S-Sun 9-6

A skull and crossbones casts a forbidding tone over this maze of merchandise. But the dealers are out to save you bucks, not pirate your pennies. With over 400 booths, you'll find treasures galore. Lots of depression glass and antique furniture. 15 booths for Western wear alone! Baby clothes (used), fishing tackle, boothes of baskets, too. Aquatic lamps at $60 are worth sailing the seven seas for. A bountiful selection that we'd gladly walk the plank after. CK, V

**NO STAR
WESTHEIMER
FLEA MARKET**
1733 Westheimer
Houston
Tel. 528-1015
T-Sun 10-6

An incredibly rude manager convinced us to scratch this one from our list. We woodn't bother with this termite's delight. Loads of furniture piled upon piles more. Knick-knacks scattered among the rest were difficult to weed out. Parking around there was no treat, either. CK

****
**WESTPARK
FLEA MARKET**
Southwest Frwy.
Westpark Exit
Houston
S-Sun 9-6

The flea in our ear was itching for us to git on over. You mite find anything here— furniture, plants, records and chickens (yup, the chick, chick kind). You'll find the parasitic bargain hunter along with those who go once in awhile, just for ticks. No way you can louse up with the multitude of choices, but prepare to elbow your way through the masses. CK

*
**WHITE ELEPHANT
FLEA MARKET**
15660 East Freeway
I-10 and Sheldon Road
Channelview
Tel. 452-9022
S-Sun 8-6

Tusk, tusk! Nothing much here to tickle the ivories. A jungle-full of plants, tools, sporting equipment. Safari we know, there are good deals to be made on ceramics, glassware and more. Truck loads of clothing that we avoided like the plague. You might find a better deal in Alabama, where the Tuscaloosa. $

FLOWERS, PLANTS, POTTERY

These alpha-bits go to the head of the class! And you won't go wrong sticking with them for plants and flowers. We saw cherry kalanchoes for $5.95, carnations for $3.95, merry mums for just $1.95, Boston ferns for $18.95 and daffy daisies for $1.95. We were gladdened over gladiolas for just $3.95-$10. Don't be leaf-ed out of the fun! CK, MC, V

****
ABC FLOWER SHOP
5856 Westheimer
Houston
Tel. 783-7455
24 hours/7 days

These plants aren't ail-en, they're healthy as can be. And quite economical as well. All these house plants are homegrown with plenty of TLC by the adorable owner. Do call before visiting and let the phone ring a while. You'll be glad to get so much of HER green for YOUR green! $

**
ALLEN'S PLANTS
1238 Bingle
Houston
Tel. 465-2427
Call first

How much does a Grecian urn? A pot full! Urn yourself a Ph.D. (doctor of phrugality) in plant-eronomics. Saving on Grecian urns and pots is the coursework and it's easy to see why B.W.'s a popular teacher. We unearthed a 13½" high Grecian urn for $7.50. Selection is limited to this one item, but you'll discover it's worth the trip to beat out un-urnthly retail prices. Call before visiting. CK

*
B. W. MATTINGLY
5711 Yale
Houston
Tel. 694-0914
M-S 9-7
(hours fluctuate)

This nursery is full of babies that won't wet on your floor or spill pablum. These organisms are healthy and happy and won't stalk your pocketbook. We couldn't leaf the Norfolk pines alone (our friend is doing five to ten for trees-tiality now—we didn't get caught). They were so tender and appealing at $3.50-$18. Veggies were just .15/ea. and a huge 6 ft. magnolia was adopted for just $9. Evergreens are ever present in the fall only. Fall for a verdant vixen. CK, MC, V

***
BEAUMONT DISCOUNT NURSERY
4625 College
Beaumont
Tel. 842-0721
M-S 9-5:30
Sun 10-5:30

There's nothing superstitious about avoiding high retail prices. It jut makes good cents. Visit this Black Cat for bewitching bargains on all manner of plantery. African violets were $3-$12, and the supply of shrubs, potting soil, indoor and outdoor plants and mulch was quite large. Check out the neat pottery line. If you buy retail, you have no one but yourself to blame for bad luck prices! CK, MC, V

**
BLACK CAT JUNK-TION
Loop 494
N. of FM 1960
Humble
Tel. 358-8461
M-S 10-5

**

**BURKHARDT'S
NURSERY**
1109 Wirt Road
Houston
Tel. 686-1821
M-S 8-5

Heart broken over rising plant prices? Relie
is in sight at Burkhardt's. We saw gorgeou
6 ft. magnolias for $15-$25. Don't climl
the walls—let their super ivy specimens do
for you! You'll encounter friendly help an
down-home prices at this oasis of value. Cl

****

CACTUS CORNER
3100 FM 1960 at
Aldine-Westfield Road
Houston
Tel. 443-2801
Sun-S 8-8:30

This cactus flower won't prick your pocket
book. You'll find bloomin' specials on al
varieties of these desert treasures, from tin
specimens to giant regiments, at graft-ifyin
prices! Their monkey grass, house plant
and ground cover all needle the competi
tion, at subterranean rates. Hanging basket
were bountiful and healthier-looking tha
Cheryl Tiegs. Don't let retail ponytails bacl
you into a corner! CK

**

CHAPMAN NURSERY
7350 N. Shepherd
Houston
Tel. 697-9165
Sun-S 8-8

We weren't chapped, man, at Chapman'
prices. Look into their hanging baskets an
see wondrous savings growing. We saw gor
geous, full baskets for $4.95-$7.95. And
you'll shout Eureka over their lovely palms
A 4 ft. specimen was $9.95 and the 20 ft
ranged $75-$100. We noticed an absence o
scheffleras. But shuffle on over and ge
tru-valu on all the rest. This man won'
chap your budget! CK

***

DISCOUNT FLOWERS
7900 Gulf Frwy.
Houston
Tel. 644-1691
M-S 9-8

Buy some red roses for your blue lady/love
for less. And tell 'em who scent-er. We wer
mellowed by the marvelous perfume of
dozen medium stem beauties for $5.9
(higher on holidays). Carnations wer
cherubic at $5.95/doz. and daisies so dea
at $2.95/bunch (16). All were fresher tha
our last blind date (and that's fresh!)
Speaking of dates, this owner always give
you the date of flowers' purchase, so i
they're old—they're free! Good for whe
the evening's going to be short anyway.

All the flowery speech of Ms. Browning's sonnets couldn't sweeten this deal any more. These magnificent examples of mums, carnations, roses and mixed bouquets are priced just right. Mums were $6.95 per plant or $3.50/bunch; carnations were .50 each or $5.95/doz. and romantic long-stemmed roses were just $10.95/doz. How do we love thee? With our pocketbooks! CK, MC, SC, V

**
THE FLOWERY
3401 Westheimer
Houston
Tel. 626-2800
M-Sun 8:30-9

Day or Knight, let one of these flora frisk up your floor-a. Fikus, schefflera and palms will stand around your place looking important for unintimidating prices. Mini palms were on sale for $20-$40, 5 ft. fikus were $19 as were 5 ft. shefflera. And hanging baskets were $8.50. Marble queen ivy was .75/4'' pot. They'll cut you in on plant cuttings to boot. Watch for sales for extra savings. $

**
**KNIGHT NURSERY
& LANDSCAPE**
2211 Pech
Houston
Tel. 465-3985
M-S 8:30-6
Sun 10-6

Open air better'n closed, Podner! This open-air market should be your target. For flower power, that is. Pick a bunch of posies for rosy prices. Carnations were $9/doz., long-stemmed roses were $21/doz., mums $3.75/bunch, daisies $3.75/bunch and orchids $7.50 and $10.50. Alas, no deliveries. But you expect a little self-service at cut-rate! CK, MC, SC, V

**
**OPEN AIR FLOWER
SHOP**
8601½ Long Point
Houston
Tel. 465-9946
M-S 9-6/Sun 10-5

This place wins palms down in the great game of plant-life. We saw a straight flush of outdoor palms for rational prices. A 15 gal. 4-6 ft. windmill variety and mediterranean fan palms were $50. Tropical plants are the house specialty (with your choice of dressing). We were fractured by frangipani for $4-$10 and plumeria was colorful at the same price. Bromeliads broke me up at $5-$25. And the terra cotta wasn't terribly costly—mostly of the large variety, though. They concentrate on exotica primarily, but you'll still find the lowly schefflera and the like. Look for an old house housing these terra firma finds. You can't stay poker-faced over wins like these! CK, MC, V

****
PALMA NURSERY
100 Avondale at Bagby
Houston
Tel. 524-7120
M-S 10-6/Sun 1-6

*
RED'S NURSERY
17831 W. Montgomery
Houston
Tel. 469-9971
M-Sun 8-6

We saw Red all right, when we tried calling several times to no avail. After nursing our wounds, we drove over and found some good prices on monkey grass $1.25 (more fun than a barrel of), ligustrum $3.50 and Japanese yew (who?) $12.50. We got prickly over the cacti at $300. CK

**
TROPICAL GARDENS
1101 Highway 6 South
Addicks
No phone listed
T-S 9-6/Th 8-5

A lawn day's journey, but bargains you won't be able to leaf alone. Petal on by for bloomin' cacti ($3.95 and up), hanging baskets $7.95 and more. No charge for close-by delivery. CK

BARGAIN OF THE MONTH

There are great times and horrible times to buy certain items. Generally, prices are lowest during the months listed below:

Dresses: January, April, June, November
Children's Clothing: July, September, November, December
Infant's Wear: January, March, April, July
Lingerie: January, May, July
Men's Clothing: August, December
Men's Shirts: January, February, July
Spring Clothes: March
Summer Clothes: June, July

Air Conditioners: February, July, August
Bathing Suits: After July 4th, August
Books: January
Cars (new): August, September
Cars (used): February, November, December
Christmas gifts: Any time but Christmas.
Curtains: February
Dishes: January, February, September
Fishing Equipment: October
Furniture: January, February, June, August, September
Hardware: August, September
Linens: January, May
Luggage: March
Party Items: December
Ski Equipment: March
Stereo Equipment: January, February, July
Television Sets: May, June
Toys: January, February
Water Heaters: January, November

FURNITURE

Surplus merchandise from their Westheimer gallery is sold here at 15-30% off. LOUIS XIV (covered in plastic) is the specialty of the house, but amidst the sea of schlock you'll find certain bargains in CENTURY, THOMASVILLE, AZZOLINI lamps and PULASKI bedroom and dining sets. A KIMBALL overstuffed chair was $250; loveseats by SORELL $299; a PULASKI curio cabinet $188 and MEMPHIS 5-pc. dinette just $74. Behold the blemishes and notice some nicks, or you may be in for a surprise when you get the stuff home. AE, SC, DC, V

**
AARON'S DISCOUNT FURNITURE
3903 Almeda
Houston
Tel. 529-3901
M-S 9-5

We got to BFO's ASAP, but after scurrying down there PDQ decided the HPD should put out an APB. No super savings on BROYHILL, SINGER, ENGLANDER or WEBB, although we did see one all-wood bedroom set for just $599. Free delivery and set-ups, but better bargains elsewhere. CK, V, MC

*
BFO FURNITURE
600 Alexander Drive
Baytown
Tel. 422-3511
M-S 9-6

These Houdinis found a way to display thousands of items in a 10' X 20' area. The magic lies in their complete photographic inventory of items they can acquire for you with their wizardry. Fine antiques (English linen press: $4900) to the most contemporary HENREDON and HERITAGE. Every couple of weeks they advertise estate sales under the "garage sale" listing in the newspaper. No sleight of hand needed here to come out with the best bargains in every furniture category. CK, MC, V

****
THE CENTER (FOR HOME FURNISHINGS INC.)
4316 Westheimer
Houston
Tel. 840-1480
M-F 10-4/S 11-3

We hoped to find Culpepper's culls, but didn't. We were hopping mad to discover the only connection between this and THE Culpepper's is their bookkeeping system. But we simmered down once we saw brand names like A. BRANDT, KING KOIL, SMITH (twin HERCULON hide-a-bed $199), WILLIAM VOLKER and STONEVILLE (5-pc. dinette set $269). Regular retail front— NOT a showroom! CK, AE, MC, V

*
CULPEPPER'S WARE-HOUSE SHOWROOM
2410 Market St.
Baytown
Tel. 427-1476
M-S 9-6

*

**DEBRUHL'S DISC.
FURNITURE MART**
Highway 146
N. of Baytown
Tel. 383-2288
T-S 9-6

Prepare to perspire in the summer and shiver in the winter as you wend your way down the narrow aisles. Squeezed in is a good selection of bedroom suites, dinette sets and sofas. KING KOIL "Wonderfirm" Queen set, usually $360 is $179 here. BROYHILL bedroom sets $699 (reg. $1099), wooden rockers for $99, dinette sets $299. Not much NODAWAY baby furniture in stock, but will order at 50% off. Delivery available for a fee, depending on mileage. MC, V

**

**DISCOUNT
FURNITURE
WAREHOUSE**
9805-M Harwin
Houston
Tel. 977-1139
M-S 10-6

Tour this promised land again this year for fare furniture buys. They'll guide you to cut-rate mattresses by SLUMBER MASTER and ENCHANTED SLEEP, as well as bedspreads to go on them. No expensive furniture was seen (as usual), but for lower-priced pieces, you can't beat 'em. CK, MC, V

*

**EXCHANGE
FURNITURE CO.**
6605 S. Rice
Bellaire
Tel. 666-0294
M-S 10-6

Exchange those retail prices for furniture you can live with. Your conscience won't wince over the savings on SERTA, SPRING AIR, ENGLANDER, BASSETT, COLLINS and MORNING GLORY. We saw a NATIONAL MOUNT AIRY repro roll top desk for $1048 (reg. $1400). All SERTA PERFECT SLEEPERS were 15% off; both new and used furniture were featured. Our faith in retailers was refunded at this Exchange. CK, MC, V

***

**4 SEASONS
FURNITURE**
8700 Stella Link
Houston
Tel. 661-0741
M-F 10-8/S 10-6

This is no May-December romance. You'll be perfectly matched to these bargains on PAUL BUNYON, HOWELL, SORELL and other name brands. We sighed over the HOWELL chrome and glass 5-pc. dinette set for $279 (reg. $449), the PAUL BUNYAN bedroom suites for $1400 (reg. $2400), the SORELL cotton quilt love seat and sofa for $699 (reg. $899). All lamps were a de-light-ful 25% off. Take advantage of their free decorating service. Go ahead. Fall for this season-ed savor and you'll come out the winter. CK, MC, V

Share a Bernhardt for much less than the old girl's worth. We saw a 9-pc. BERN-HARDT dining set for $997 (reg. $2200). We got SEALY over the large stock of mattresses selling for a song, and hounded them for the BASSETT 6-pc. bedroom suite at $399 (reg. $799). All these goodies are repos, discontinueds, slightly damaged or obviously abused, but if you choose carefully, you can take home a pro for non-union prices. THAYER-COGGIN merchandise was 60% off, but in short, short supply. This Fingers outlet thumbs its nose at retail—and you will too. CK, MC, V

**
**FURNITURE
CLEARANCE CTR.**
2200 Jefferson
Houston
Tel. 228-0082
M-S 10-6

This hunk had some of the best lines we'd seen. We were panting over the HENRE-DON, PEMKAY, CARLTON, BAKER and HICKORY TAVERN. And the best ones are older, you know. Like the luscious English antiques. From sofas to Bombay chest, we admired their attributes. They run those marvelous ads for super sales, so keep your eyes peeled. CK, AE, MC, V

****
**FURNITURE
CLEARANCE CTR.**
730 Town & Country
Houston
Tel. 461-4681
M-Th 10-9/S 10-6

For HICKORY, dicker at the dock. We also saw BASSETT, MERSMAN, ASHLEY and SINGER. They handled damaged freight furniture and offered prices that would have made our heart soar. We saw a HICKO-RY love seat and sofa for $359 (reg. $595), a MERSMAN glass topped table for $74.50 (reg. $179), a BASSETT French Provincial antique white bedroom set with queen headboard and triple dresser for $673 (reg. $995) and oriental lamps at $36 (reg. $59). The price on the BASSETT bedroom suite at $789 (reg. $1295) was nifty. $

***
**FURNITURE
WAREHOUSE CO.**
1810 Franklin
Houston
Tel. 228-2020
M-F 8-5:30/S 8-5

With what this Gardner is shoveling, everything's coming up roses. But the flagrant fragrance (?) of a snotty attitude got to us. Considering their lines are middle of the road anyway, we wouldn't rush over unless you're wearing knee (hip) boots. They carry WYMAN LLOYD, GLOBE, HICKO-RY and GILLIUM, but not to extremes. A modest discount indeed was seen. CK, MC, SC, V

*
GARDNER SALES
2504 Amherst
Houston
Tel. 526-4551
M-F 9-5/S 9-5:30

**NV
GILLIAN FURNI-
TURE RENTAL CO.
WAREHOUSE SALE**
5704 Southwest Frwy.
Houston
Tel. 785-5100
M, Th 9-8/T-W 9-6
F 9-5/S 9-3

Drowning in a sea of high-priced furniture? Gillian's island is an atoll of value for the weary of wallet. Native to this warehouse were sofas for $100, chairs for $40 and dinette sets for $75-$150. We saw KING KOIL doubles for $55. They stock ten dinettes in the showroom at all times and five bedroom sets. Also, rent a living room, bedroom, dining set for as low as $49/mo. When it comes to retail, it's sink or swim. Catch this raft of savings. CK

****
**HOUSTON
CONSUMER CENTER**

See write-up under "Buying Services." (New Listings Section)

***
**HOWELL'S DISC.
FURNITURE**
2070 Gulf St.
Beaumont
Tel. 832-2544
M-S 10-6

How-well d'you like a bargain? We thought so, or you wouldn't have shelled out $3.95 for this book. We Howell'd over a SUPE-RIOR 5-pc. living room suite for $398 (reg. $495), ALLEN WHITE swivel rockers for $139, MASSOUD rockers for $229 and vinyl sofas for $299. You'll also find BROYHILL, BENCHCRAFT, BASSETT and THOMASVILLE worthy of a scream. There's a $10 minimum delivery charge. How-ell do you spell savings? Ver-r-y carefully! CK, MC, V

*
**IMPERIAL DISCOUNT
HOME CENTER**
1895 College
Beaumont
Tel. 833-3149
M-S 9-6

This Imperial seems to be pure cane sham. Quick-dissolving discounts are dubious on already low-end priced furniture. KING KOIL was one of the featured brands but they refused to reveal their revered mark-up. We received rude treatment from her Royal Highness, then were told they have great prices. No horse trader is going to point out missing teeth. Who's to believe? MC, V GECC

**
**JOE'S FURNITURE
SHOWROOM**
2600 Calder
Beaumont
Tel. 838-3753
M-S 9-6

Discounts at Joe's were fair. We saw genuine mis-matched king-size mattresses for $98, discount matching for $198 (reg. $249), PAUL BUNYAN bedroom suites were $995 (reg. $1495), BROYHILL dining 8-pc. set was $950 (reg. $1300), AWALT recliners were $79, BENCHCRAFT queen-size sleeper was $399 (reg. $479). We apologize to Joe for printing in last year's book that this was an ex-porn theater. We've just learned that it was a bowling alley. Now you be good boys and girls and don't go on strike. CK, MC, V

Leave it to Levitz—the only furniture outlet that's ON the tracks, instead of across them. Their famous after-the-sale service has won them friends and influenced competitors. We saw a CARTER 10-pc. pit group (sounds like fun) for $1700 (reg. $2300), an INTERNATIONAL sofa and loveseat duo was $1000 (reg. $1300). Delivery takes 3-4 days. By the way, don't whip out your plastic money. They've rail-roaded credit mongers. Toot, Toot! CK, GECC

LEVITZ FURNITURE
OUTLET
1009 Brittmore
Houston
Tel. 461-2340
M-S 10-9/Sun 10-9
Sun Browing

Don't get mad, get plaid. This Scotchman will save you all the money he clan. Wee lass-oed a WHIRLPOOL washer/dryer combo for $519, an 18,000 BTU air conditioner for $469, a SUPERIOR sofa, loveseat and chair for $369, and their vinyl couch and chair for $399 kilt the competition! They even unloaded VISA and MASTER CHARGE to sav-u-mor. Thrifty McLaury's no bag of wind! CK

MCLAURY'S
FURNITURE AND
APPLIANCES
Fourth and College
Beaumont
Tel. 832-4591
M-F 9:15-6/S 9:30-4

Is there such a thing as bankruptcy insurance? These folks ought to check it out. Not only were the sales force S-L-O-W on the uptake, but the appliance prices might as well have had balls and chains! They'll never move very fast at this no-bargain rate. None are stocked. The owner journeys to the distributor for your desired. We saw a used stove for $89 and used sofas were so-so at $50-$100. How anxious to sell can someone be who doesn't even open on Saturday? CK

NEIGHBORHOOD
FURNITURE
1012 Telephone
Houston
Tel. 921-2168
M-F 9-5

Mama Mia! Let Pasadena inter-ven-a! You can save cashola with this go-between-a you and high prices. They still tout 35-58% off retail, same as we tol' ya last year. And we saw good supporting evidence. Overstuffed (like Mama's manicotti) recliners were $174 in Herculon, $99 in vinyl. S & K wooden dinettes were $259, the five pieces. We also gorged on RIVERSIDE, STYLEHOME, FOX, STRATO and HARRIS bellissimo buys. AND they've air-conditioned since last year! CK, MC

PASADENA FURN.
BARGAIN BARN
1216 S. Center
Pasadena
Tel. 473-1903
T-S 10-5

FURTURE

**

RATTAN BUDGET SHOP
11135 Gulf Frwy.
Houston
Tel. 941-1660
M-S 10-5:30

A rodent on the Riviera can get a rattan. A better Rattan is the Rattan Budget Shop. We shot down high-priced rattan with great buys from here. We witnessed gangs of zingers in first grade, discontinueds, slightly damaged and one-of-a-kind stock. Saw a queen-size headboard for $98, trunks (better than Dumbo's) for $50/$165 and divider screens for $165. All at 10-15% off retail. Y-o-u-u dirty rat, you. CK, MC, SC, V

**

RIDGECREST FURNITURE
8312 Long Point
Houston
Tel. 468-2686
T-F 10-6/S 10-5

Whoever said "Home Sweet Home" didn't have to pay today's prices to furnish it. Sweeten your hearth and home with 15-20% off on HICKORY, SERTA, STANLEY, BASSETT, BROYHILL and STRATO-LOUNGER. They're still selling their great fabric for 20% off. And their decorating divas do wonders with arranging in your abode. Free delivery makes this a bargain that takes the "loan" out of home. CK, MC, V

*

STERLING FURNITURE
5904-A N. Shepherd
Houston
Tel. 695-7039
M-F 9-6/S 9-5

Their sterling qualities are somewhat suspect. After we found they'd terminated free delivery (it's now a whopping $18-$25) we terminated the dialogue. But they still carry BASSETT and SINGER and offer a discount off retail. CK, MC, SC, V

**

SUNILAND CLEARANCE CTR.
7301 Clarewood Dr.
Houston
Tel. 774-8711
M, Th 10-9/T-S 10-6

This Suniland Express whooshes through town with windfall savings. We saw great RIVERSIDE, BENCHCRAFT and HICKORY furniture for 20-50% off regular retail. All aboard for the floor models, samples, discontinueds and odds and evens from Suniland's "regular" store. We were headed in the right direction with the DREXEL headboards from $39 up. Give your furniture budget a ca-boost with these engineious buys. CK

Lamp askew? Bentwood bent? Sofa sagging? For furniture complaints, contact:

> **Southern Furniture Manufacturers' Assocation**
> **235 South Wrenn**
> **High Point, NC 27261**
> **Tel. (919) 889-1905**

GIFTWARE

Jump around, turn around, and pick from a glorious collection of designer looks in home furnishings and giftware. Meet your new friends and change your outlook at home. Fabric, wall coverings, drapery, pillows, accessories, furniture and a basket boutique of bargains (best prices in town), combined to achieve an eclectic menagerie of decorator know-how. Create your house beautiful look at down-home prices. Great-looking lamps begin at $45. Visit also Changing Look and Friends, 5413 Bellaire Blvd. at Chimney Rock, Tel. 669-0921. CK, MC, V

***
THE CHANGING LOOK
3638 University
Houston
Tel. 661-3015
M-F 10-6/Th 10-9
S 10-4

One of Dee best deals we've seen on collectibles. Really interesting gifts. $

**
DEE'S ATTIC
8027 Brockbank
Houston
Tel. 641-4364
Call for hours

Feeling like the morning after? You can't beat Tuesday Morning for a quick pick-you-up. Our eyes were opened to heavy savings on FITZ & FLOYD, GEORGE BRIARD, AUDREY and SCHOTT crystal. Copperware, dinnerware, planters, bar glasses, place mats, napkins, wicker baskets, ski jackets, suede clothing . . . whew! We could go on and on. But you'll have to go on over to see for yourself what fine merchandising really is. Scheduled for four sales per year, these were the dates to watch for: Sept. 15-Oct. 15, Thanksgiving thru Christmas, March 1-April 1 and June 1-July 1. A morning here is like a week's vacation! Check directory for other locations. CK, MC, V

NR
TUESDAY MORNING
Westbury Square
Houston
Tel. 729-2220
Sept. 15-Oct. 15
Thanksgiving-Christmas
March 1-April 1
June 1-July 1

Tired of the Pier-I Monkey-pod Syndrome? Get into the world of walnut for ½ price. Old Hickory and his troops could've had a walnut salad bowl (to serve six) for $14; eaten by the light of walnut candlesticks for $3.15-$5.80; nibbled from nut dishes for $4.70-$16.75/set of six; played taps in a walnut ashtray for $3-$6.85 or brought home lazy Susan for $10. Pickle your own barrel for $14.50 full size, $8 for ½ size. CK, MC, V

*
WALNUT BOWL FACTORY STORE 5
Rt. 1 (I-35E)
Hillsboro
Tel. 582-9068
Summer 8-8 (Sun-S)
Winter 8-6 (Sun-S)

HANDCRAFTED ITEMS

*
**ARTISAN II
FASHIONS**
1731 Westheimer
Houston
Tel. 523-0809
T-Sun 11-6

We saw veils of blue at Artisan II, plus many more very interesting goodies. Such as an antique Afghanistan dress made from veils—for just $59; 1940's pure silk Chinese dresses were $110; 100-yr. old COPTIK Ethiopian crosses were $30; Indian huraches were $7. We saw an "ought-3" solid bronze cash register for $1500 (that should ring up interest at a party) and lots of '30s costume jewelry. CK, CB, MC, DC, V

*
**AUNTY'S HOPE
CHEST**
2042 FM 1960
Houston
Tel. 440-7202
M-S 9:30-5

We've been hoping on our chests for years and haven't grown an inch! Regardless, we CAN add to our kitchen dimensions with pot holders, place mats and spice ropes. All kinds of knick-knacks are rick-racked for your inspection. Most are placed on consignment by little old ladies. We saw afghans for $20-$300 (reg. $60 and up). Quilts and pillowcases, too. CK, MC, V

*
**UNA-UNICEF
CHARITY GIFT SHOP**
77 Woodlake Square
Houston
Tel. 783-7382
M-S 10-5/Th 10-9

Charity begins at home with these far-flung treasures 'n pleasures. You'll discover rugs, ceramics, cards, etc. We donated glances to worldly baskets, from $4-$20; a leather tribal milk jug from Borana was $40; Peruvian blankets were $75; Mexican potteries were $5 and up and boxes of UNICEF cards were $2. CK, MC, V

HEALTH FOODS

,,*
**GENERAL
NUTRITION CENTER**
402 Gulfgate Mall
Houston
Tel. 649-9753
M-F 10-9/S 10-7

General Nutrition, leader of the bod squad, says "Don't be ill—pop a pill." Vitamins A thru E are furnished, and these troops will advise on which is for what. Healthy discounts are had on special sales, so watch the Sunday paper and in-store flyers that wing your way. We're sure their herb teas and wholesome foods will please. Let their basic training start you on the road to winning the health war! CK, MC, V

HOME IMPROVEMENT

Is your lumber dollar going down the sewer? Channelview-er! More for your mon, hon, in tools, woods and paints. We saw-ed off No. 2 grade cedar fencing for $2.27/post (1" X 6" X 6'). At least 60 different sheets of paneling pummeled our senses. We chose 4' X 8' masonite sheets for $3.95/ea. And 4' X 8' laminated wood for $6.75. Their SKIL tools are abundant—and tho they don't advertise discount, they have lower mark-up than regular retail. Don't funnel your dollars down the drain when you can tunnel them toward a gain! CK, MC, V

*
**CHANNELVIEW
DISC. LUMBER YARD**
16120 Market St.
Channelview
Tel. 452-7133
M-F 7:30-5:30
S 7:30-1

As our friend Mork always says, building materials used to cost hundred of gleebs. And tools were out of this galaxy! But we know this place always gives at least 10% off on paint, lumber, roofing, bricks and electrical supplies. Shazbat! We forgot to tell you they have discount tools, too. Now get out there and give it all the krepzat you've got! Don't be a nimnul. CK

*
**DISCOUNT LUMBER
AND SUPPLY CO.**
117 Oakdale
Liberty
Tel. 336-5948
M-S 9-5:30

Dis' count the hundreds of bargains. They have wounded retailers for miles around with their consistent bargains on wallpaper, lumber goods, light bulbs, shingles and tools. Builders frequent this spot but their prices are still the same as for the little guy. Which warms our hearts. CK, MC, V

**
**DISCOUNT LUMBER
MART**
3901 Airline
Houston
Tel. 697-2773
M-F 8-8/S 8-5

The South is rising—on Dixie ladders. This Dixie-land band o' savings will fine tune your discount on step-stools and ladders. Builders know and love this pea-pickin' savin' place. Most things are 30-40% off retail and that ain't hay. Most of their ladders are commercial heavy-weight, but they will special-order a lightweight at FULL discount just for you! You can't beat that with Ma's pine switch! CK

***
DIXIE LADDER CO.
9501 Monroe Road
Houston
Tel. 991-2688
M-F 7:30-5/S 7:30-12

Tired of lumbering all over town to find cheap wood? They'll shorten your search (and your 1" X 12", too, if you're not careful). This No. 84 was stocked with 10' 2" X 4"s for $1.84; 1" plywood decking (4' X 8') was $7.19 and paneling ran $4.99-$13. All wood is No. 2 grade. Watch for special sales when you can really rack up the shavings! CK

**
84 LUMBER
5801 610 S. Loop
Crestmont Exit
Houston
Tel. 734-2684
M-F 8-8/S-Sun 8-5

**
**FACTORY CABINET
& APPLIANCE CO.**
7317 Almeda Road
Houston
Tel. 747-6923
M-F 9-5/Th 9-8
S 9:30-1

Jimmy Carter could have gotten a new cabinet a lot easier here. We found we could staff our kitchen, bathroom or workshop with our own design or select from lovely floor models. We saw 25% off on most items. Is your vanity no longer fair? They'll supply you with a glowing new marble top, cut to fit. Sinks and recessed lighting available, too. CK

*
**LACKS WHOLESALE
DISTRIBUTORS**
6867 Wynnwood
Houston
Tel. 861-9941
M-F 10-8/S 9-6

They Lack-ed luster, but who cares. We found spice for our leisure life at this distribution point. We saw stereos, TV's, sporting goods out the raft and all manner of hardware for those week-end putterers. A huge selection beckoned and friendly sales folk didn't make resisting any easier. We decided to turn lazy hours into constructive powers with the right equipment for less! CK, MC, V

*
**MANUFACTURER'S
SURPLUS OUTLET**
9712 Old Katy Road
Houston
Tel. 932-0263
M-F 9-7/Sun 10-5

We directed you into this outlet last year. And we still think they deserve a look-see. Tools and hardware were priced hot-to-go and gew-gaws 'n doo-dads had real drive-in appeal. We spotted tableware, trash cans and paper goods, for about 1/3 to 1/2 off. If you've got more time than money, scoot on out. CK, MC, V

***
OLSHAN'S
2600 Commerce
Houston
Tel. 225-5551
M-F 7:30-5
S 7:30-4:30

Same ol' shan, passing out bargains, fast as he can. His hardware supplies enjoy a fame of their own. They're still running those great TRU-TEST paint specials we told you about last year. So watch your daily. They replaced their catalogue with a 6-page booklet, but we still got all the facts. These folks come by their lower prices thru volume buying. And you'll come by savings thru their front door! CK, MC, V

****
**RURAL PLUMBING
SUPPLIES & SERVICE**
14506 Hempstead Hwy.
Houston
Tel. 460-9968
M-S 8-5

We went plumb nuts when we found their bargains. We found new, slightly scratched tubs for $15 that left us drained from excitement. Colored CRANE Grand Prix tubs were $89, and bar sinks set up at $25 (reg. $54). Saw commodes by GALAXY, CRANE and BIGGS that take a back seat to none, John. Won't get caught in hot water with 40 gallon electric hot water heaters for $109.95 or 40 gallon gas for $119.95. MC, V

We will Grant, General Lee, that Southland is a good place to shop. Last year we told you about their auto accessories, kitchenware, housewares, hardware and decorating doo-dads. They're all still here in volume, much like a great big country store. They were cheap on HANDY HARDWARE water-base latex paint—just $7.88/gal. We saw other bargain buys as well. Shop for yourself and surrender to savings. CK, MC, V

*
SOUTHLAND HARDWARE
1822 Westheimer
Houston
Tel. 529-4743
M-S 8-6

The remodeling business is mushrooming, and the fruit of the boom is Strawberry's. Berry retail prices under six feet of discount. Venture into this back room grotto of bargain magic and you'll come out with 50% off most patterns of wallpaper. These are discontinued wallpapers that were running $1-$8/roll when we were in. So ignore the over 300 books of selections in front. CK, MC, V

**
STRAWBERRY REMODELING AND SUPPLIES
1915 Strawberry
Pasadena
Tel. 473-8291
M-F 8-8/S 9-4

Tower Iron Works—but not as good as champagne and roses. Are you a person of iron grill? Hold your own with high prices on locks, gates, bars, grills, spiral staircases and balconies. Tower will attempt to work from your custom design, but don't push it. They generally prefer to go with the tried 'n true. Prices ran about 20% off. CK, V

*
TOWER IRON WORKS
2322 Bissonnet
Houston
Tel. 527-0477
M-F 8-4:30/S 8-12

JEWELRY

The way house prices have shot up lately, we don't see how a Diamond Palace could cost much more. We found great deals on diamonds, jewels and gold! The king's special treat was still the $49.95 diamond earrings that regularly retail for $99 or more (no increase since we reported to you last year). We were entertained by the 15" gold chains for $25 and gold bracelets from $17-$35. The goodies are made here and all sell from 30-60% off retail. And yes, they still take trade-ins. This ice palace keeps you warm when cold retail winds blow. Other location at 2811 Fondren Road. CK, AE, DC, MC, V

**
DIAMOND PALACE
11047 Northwest Frwy.
Deauville Plaza
Houston
Tel. 680-1924
M-S 10-6/F 10-8

JEWELRY

***
FINESSE JEWELERS
8300 Southwest Frwy.
Houston
Tel. 776-0577
M-S 10-6/Th 10-7

A Finesse a fishy arm. It is also a great jeweler. They design and execute their glorious creations right here on the premises, thereby saving us Shoppers beaucoups of capital. Very friendly and accommodating, these owners are such gems they made us WANT to give them our jewelry money! Gold and platinum are still a specialty and they mount, remount and repair as ever. Let them add a little polish to your life! CK, AE, MC, V

***
14 KT. CONNECTION
5555 W. Loop South
Suite 472
Bellaire
Tel. 669-0979
M-F 10-4:30
S by appt. only

Eh-h-h, wanna know what's up, Doc? These karats go for garden-patch prices when compared to many local retailers. Gold bracelets started at $13 (14-18K), delicate chains were $16, charms were just $6 and stickpins were $29. When we dug for our lettuce and came up short, they offered their 90-day layaway plan. Don't forget to take a pot shot at their marvelous rings, too. They started at a tasty $20. Don't let some nit-wit wabbit fool you into retail prices. Be-Fudd-le him! CK, V, MC

*
GIGI JEWELRY
2443 University Blvd.
Houston
Tel. 527-0819
M-S 10-6

GiGi, you've been growing up before our very eyes. Have we been standing up too close to see your charming 18" ivory beads for $60? Or your 18" carved pineapple necklace for $75? What mouthwatering lapis beads you had for $130 and your malachite necklace for $75 was endearing. Turquoise and sterling were featured tempters as well. With virtues like these, we'll stay forever young at heart! Other stores under different names at Northwest and Almeda Malls (The Bombay Shops, Ltd.) and Memorial Mall (Concho Jewelry). CK, DC, MC, V

****
HERFORT DIAMOND RING FACTORY
2200 Avenue H
Rosenberg
Tel. 342-2542
M-S 9-6/Th 9-9

This Herfort gives you more for your moo-ney. We cow-culated 50% savings. Besides getting diamonds at this bargain price, we saw some of the lowest prices we ever herd of on rubies, emeralds, sapphires. Most rings we saw were already mounted, but they've got plenty of loose stones, too. They'll be glad to show you the best way to care for your purchases. CK

114

See write-up under "Buying Services." (New Listings Section)

Just like the other Jaycees, these guys are do-gooders. They guided us in the purchase of precious stones without cutting us on the sharp edge of high prices. Over a half-million dollars worth of rocks call Sloan's home. Buying directly from the diamond cutters in Belgium and Israel cut us in on the lower prices. They're expanding nation-wide to flout their CLOUT! Other location at 6110 Westheimer. CK, AE, CB, DC, MC, SC, V

This ol' factory smells like a winner. We saw genuine craftsmen, in the tradition of quality. They said we could design our own or trust them. (Where have we heard that before?) Repairs and remounting were offered, but they've deleted engraving from their docket since we went to press last year. We glimpsed gorgeous gold chains from $28 (for a 15"). They also worked sterling into stylish sensations. CK, MC

Lewis, Nathan but the best is what we saw. We found you very serious about trying to sell for less. Plenty of gold and diamond jewelry but most was already "set." They sold for reasonable prices, lower than one or two ritzy stores in town. Their SAMSONITE was regular price unless they're unloading discontinued colors—in which case, they're 1/3 off. CK, MC, V, AE

This Reiner's no meat-head. He had super strong savings on SAMSONITE. First quality SAMSONITE was 25% off and discontinued colors were 35% off. Gold and diamond jewelry are also featured for "negotiable" prices. (On the surface they seem retail. But you know about looks being deceiving. Look at Delilah.) Over 150 different mountings await your perusal. Drop by and try your might at crushing retail prices. CK, MC, V

****
HOUSTON CONSUMER CENTER

*
J. C. SLOAN
811 Dallas Ave.
Houston
Tel. 654-0990
M, Th 9:30-8:30
T-S 9:30-5:30

*
JEWELRY FACTORY
4114 Decker Dr.
Baytown
Tel. 424-7331
M-S 9-5:30

*
LEWIS-NATHAN JEWELRY CO.
420 Main
Houston
Tel. 222-2381
M-S 9-5:30

*
REINER'S JEWELRY STORE
412 Main
Houston
Tel. 227-3907
M-S 9:30-6

****
**STANDARD WHOLE-
SALE JEWELERS**
705 Main, 2nd floor
Houston
Tel. 227-8989
M-F 9:30-5
Closed for lunch from
1:30-2:30

The Standard Operating Procedure here was DISCOUNT. We had a great time checking the 25-50% off on BULOVA and SEIKO watches. With 35 years in business, Standard's fine reputation preceeds them. Rings, bracelets and chains charmed us into submission. We will wear them with flair to our vanity fair. And there's no red tape to tie up your bureau-ocracy. This lovely gold jewelry at lower than retail prices will bring us back. CK

LAPIDARY SUPPLIES

***
**BRYDON'S
LAPIDARY SUPPLY**
1503 Zora
Houston
Tel. 686-6014
M, W-S 9:30-5

Lapidary doesn't mean a fast run around the cow barn. It is the art of gem cutting and polishing. This supplier will special order crafters' needs at 5-20% off retail. Work with 22 gauge sterling wire for .40/ft. (at last check). His SWEST, TSI and H&R quality supplies bring 'em in from miles around. Don't get stoned here, though. His tools, wax castings and wire were good buys, but precious rocks were still overpriced. CK

*
KING'S GEM CENTER
5510 North Frwy.
Houston
Tel. 694-7219
M-W, F 9:30-6
Th 9:30-8/S 9:30-4

This King Solomon-ly mines the store. We finally quit fretting around, trying to dig up gold and jewels for next-to-nothing. We saved dollars royally with do-it-yourself supplies. Their 12-week intensive silversmith course made it easy. Don't miss the big selection of how-to books. They also featured rocks and fossils to dabble with. Gem-i-ny Cricket! CK, V, MC

LIGHTING AND LAMPS

Lighten your load of lamp bills. In updating last year's visit, we still found NATIONAL, ACME, CAMBRIDGE and IMPERIAL for 30% off. But the back room is the star re-turn engagement. You're on the right track with TRACK LIGHTING KING—all 10% off. The sales help were all de-light-ful and the owner's charm is truly incandescent! Be sure to turn on to their other locations: 7219 Bissonnet, 1818 FM 1960 West and 1013-A Dairy Ashford. CK, MC, V

Have we got a flash for you! These enlightened fix-teurs turn up a 35% discount on all their illuminators. We were blinded by the TIFFANY repros for $84-$400. L&S strip lighting with large bulbs was $40 (reg. $60); recessed, flourescent and track lighting was going for the contract price—35% off retail (including HALO tracks). A dazzling array of dizzying prisms from the chandeliers shouldn't keep you from seeing the great desk and floor lamps. The 7320 Southwest Freeway locale has lots of doo-dads like silk flowers and dried arrangements. Let this be your very own Age of Enlightenment! CK, AE, SC, MC, V

See write-up under "Buying Services." (New Listings Section)

Don't hide your light under a bushel of re-tail prices. Shine up to savings on track lights, closeouts, discontinueds, samples and knock-offs. We saw a racy 30% off track lighting and 50% off pieces the owner does not modify. We also sorted out many styles, including floor, desk and hanging models, as well as accessories such as shades. At least a 100 watt stop! CK, MC, V

A-J's was O. K. with
**
A & O LAMP REPAIR
6715 Wesleyan at
Bellaire Blvd.
Houston
Tel. 664-3129
M-F 9-6/S 9-5

***
**DISCOUNT
FIXTURES, INC.**
1211 S. Loop West
Houston
Tel. 748-7212
M-F 8-6/Th 8-9/S 9-6

****
**HOUSTON
CONSUMER CENTER**

**
**SOUTHWESTERN
LAMP CO.**
9941 Rowlett
Houston
Tel. 946-1235
M-S 10-6/Th 10-9

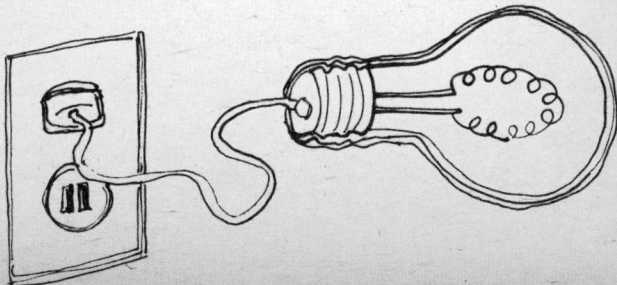

LIQUOR, WINE AND SPIRITS

*
**A-J'S DISCOUNT
LIQUOR STORES**
3222 Calder
Beaumont
Tel. 835-5931
M-S 10-8

A-J's was O. K. with us. We bellied on up to a barful of bargains on wine and liquors. Our spirits were raised (as well as our price-consciousness) by the TANQUERAY gin $6.89/fifth. MOET & CHANDON was $18.69 for the 1973 vintage. We found we could purchase a case and get 12 bottles for the price of 10. They run special-er specials on Friday and Saturday, so watch your daily. We understand that the Royal Butcher, Sir Rowsis of Liver, shops there. $

MATERNITY

**
**MATERNITY
FACTORY OUTLET**
6363 Westheimer
Houston
Tel. 780-0919
M, Th 10-9
T-W, F-S 10-6

It ain't nec-caesarean-ly so. You don't have to search high and low to find 25% off on stylish storklothes. These DAN HOWARD pants, dresses, tops, bathing suits, etc., were straight from the factory to you. We saw $18 pants for $13 and bathing suits were $15-$40. Plenty of dressing room for the modest. Buying maternity togs at cut-rate won't cut down on baby's quality. CK, MC, V

MENSWEAR

**
BARRY MFG.
7280 Wynnwood
Houston
Tel. 861-4015
M, Th-S 9-6/T-W 9-9

These folks are still Barry-ing glad tidings to artificial fiber lovers. We saw "straight from the Georgia factory" specials like 3-pc. suits for $62 and cotton and poly raincoats for $39. Wide size range from 35-58. We didn't see a 100%-er in the lot—all synthetic blends offered. For those who aren't afraid of a constant diet of polyesters. CK, MC, V

The last time we went through a door with "Men's" written on it, our face got flushed. Well, "Men's" is right. No boy's items here. We saw men's FLORSHEIM, NUNN-BUSH and FREEMAN tootsie-tempters. Check out the men's pants, Orson, which run to size 60! We'd heard that their jeans prices were blue-ti-ful. Only for those with a hankering for local-yokel labels, however. Still, some bargains to be had for the careful Discount Shop-per. CK, MC, V

*
MEN'S DISCOUNT SHOP
1020 N. 11th St.
Beaumont
Tel. 832-4488
M-W, S 9-6/Th-F 9-8

This wearhouse is a men's room on the rise. Stock keeps improving! Cut-out labels were the rule for $79-$175 suits. The owner tells us he's dropped the overseas/Iron Curtain models and has gone American on us. We saw a few leftover Rumanian designs, but they'll probably still be leftover when we open LBJ's time capsule. We see potential here and advise you to stay a-double-breast of the situation. CK, MC, V

**
THE MEN'S WAREHOUSE
9311 Katy Frwy.
Houston
Tel. 932-6296
M-F 10-9/S 9:30-6

The only bad thing about this store was that it carried only men's clothes. Our heads were reeling from all the labels—HART, SCHAFFNER AND MARX, PARKE, HASPEL, COUNT LIDO, HATHAWAY, NORRIS, GANT—and oh, those double-ply, full-fashioned cashmeres for only $39, sports coats for $39, HASPEL poplin suits for $79, and PIERRE CARDIN, JOHNNY CARSON and PALM BEACH suits for $89.50! The attentive personnel will help you find quality merchandise through the classification system—X is lowest quality, which improves with the numbers 1 through 6. They told us that a discount of 40% and up was standard, so you can keep your husbands and sons well-dressed, and save enough to shop the rest of the stores in The Underground Shopper! CK

****
MERCHANT'S WHOLESALE EXCHANGE
1401 Fannin
Houston
Tel. 659-1876
M-F 9-5:30/S 9-3

119

★★★★
SAAD'S TAILOR
3231 Fondren
Houston
Tel. 780-8833
M-F 9-7/S 9:30-5

We saw the best imaginable bargains in quality men's clothing. Custom suits in exquisite fabrics could be had for $275 and up. Some custom suits don't get picked up (like Cousin LaVinia in the single's bar). Well, when that happens, Saad hangs them on the rack at LOW prices and sells them first come, first served. We saw discounts on GIVENCHY silk shirts and ROLAND ties, too. Saad's is tailor made for the shopper with the tasteful eye. CK, MC, V

★
SIMON MFG. CO.
6541 Southwest Frwy.
Houston
Tel. 774-3378
M-F 9-9/S 9-6

Sigh, mon cherie. You won't find much that is appetizing on this manufacturer's menu. Still peddling their label-less suits for less, alright. And ties and sportcoats are served up a la carp. Gourmet fare it wasn't. You'll still see the Rumanian specials and polyester potpourri. But they're more like c-rations than tasty temptations. Or maybe it was just us. Maybe they really ARE the fashionable, incredibly su-ave clothiers they'd have us believe??? Na-a-a-a. Visit other locations: 9540 Hempstead; Men's Suits Unlimited at 6445 Westheimer; and Palm Center Menswear at 5259 Palm Center. CK, AE, CB, MC, V

★★★
THE TAILORS
8936 Clarkcrest
Houston
Tel. 781-6300
M-S 10-6

Want a tailor-made thrill? Call this owner and just listen to him TALK! Four stars for the sexiest voice in Houston! Now, getting down to business (a-hem!), we saw suits by GIVENCHY, AUGUSTUS, DON ROBBI, CERRUTI, CARDIN and TALLIA for less mark-up than one would find in most retail establishments. You'll love their attentive alterations—they're so-o detailed minded! Hey fella, won't you send us a tape to listen to on cold, lonesome nights? Retail store located at 6360 Richmond. CK, MC, V

PLEASE, MR. POSTMAN

Avoid the Gloom of Night when Buying by Mail

1. Check the company's reputation before placing an order. The Better Business Bureau won't recommend a firm, but they will tell you if they've had any complaints about the FLY BY NIGHT DOODAD COMPANY.

2. Read descriptions carefully. "Marble-toned" is not marble, "mink-type" generally means plastic fur, and beware simulated anything.

3. Don't be disappointed if the product doesn't look like the picture. (Think of your driver's license, and be grateful!)

4. Keep a record of the date you ordered, important numbers, the phone number and address of the company. "Sometime in March . . . or maybe it was September . . ." doesn't help them find your order.

5. Send a check or money order ONLY. This is your proof of purchase.

6. Write your name, address, and any special instructions clearly. Mrs. Squiggle Squiggle of Squiggle Street, Squiggle, Texas NEVER gets any good mail.

7. Know the firm's return policy. Assume nothing.

8. Shipping charges can double the price of some goods, especially air freight. A $2 music box is no bargain if the shipping charges are $15.

9. Be realistic about delivery dates. Too many people order Christmas gifts in November, and wonder why the stuff doesn't come down the chimney on schedule.

10. If you have a complaint regarding mail order service or practice, write to the MAIL ORDER ACTION LINE, 6 East 43rd Street, New York, NY 10017.

MOVIES

**
GARDEN OAKS THEATER
3750 N. Shepherd
Houston
Tel. 692-5036
Call for show times
M-Sun

Wanna be scared outa your wit's-you-call-it? This marvelous $1 movie house runs such fare as "Screams of a Winter Night" (ooh, Ma, where's my Mickey night light?). They even have a Bella Lugosi sound-alike giving recorded times and features on the phone. Refreshments and games make the bargain even juicier . . . Booga-Booga! $

***
LONG POINT CINEMA
10016 Long Point
Houston
Tel. 468-7948
Call for show times

Double your pleasure and your money's worth with these two-fers: two recent movies for the price of one low-down dollar. Get your feet stuck to the floor, your sleeves stuck to the chair arms and your teeth stuck in Milk Duds. It's all in an afternoon's fun. $

MUSICAL INSTRUMENTS

***
ELEVENTH STREET DISCOUNT MUSIC
65 N. 11th St.
Beaumont
Tel. 833-9456
M-F 8:30-5:30

We were saved at the eleventh hour by this eleventh street music-man. Sweet owner socked us real rag-time bargains on KAWAI pianos, a brand in which he believes 100%. We were quoted $1995 on a super console (reg. $2795), $3795 on an ebony grand (reg. $6000) and $1095 on a beautiful organ (reg. $1395). You'll sing the praises of their free delivery. This nice proprietor will arrange a private appointment at YOUR convenience to discuss saving YOUR money! What class. CK

**
FREEMAN'S PIANO WAREHOUSE
6101 Pinemont
Houston
Tel. 683-9221
M, Th 9:30-9
T-S 9:30-6

Free, man, they ain't! But we've seen worse. We saw a new AEOLIAN spinet for $795 (reg. $1195); a new 2-keyboard organ was $795 (reg. $1295), a used KAWAI grand was $895, a used practice piano was $195 and a used HAMMOND organ was $495 (reg. $895). No need to plead guilty to retail prices. Overpower nasty big-time piano pedal-ers today. Other location at 6310 Gulf Freeway. CK, HOUSEHOLD FINANCE, REPUBLIC NATIONAL BANK

OFFICE FURNITURE AND EQUIPMENT

We were sure glad we didn't wait till December 24 to go Carroll-ing this year! Lots of good buys on new and used office furniture. Saw a tan legal size filing cabinet (used) with four drawers for $99 and a used metal desk (24" X 54") for $119. Florescent lamps were shining on at $38. CK

Sitting behind a desk all day would be a little easier if your desk came from The Desk Factory. Everything they offered was custom made with lots of class to fit your . . . job. All wood secretarial desks were $499-$1000. Steno chairs ranged from $59-$99 which prompted us to take a seat. Other locations at 4611 Fannin, 1400 Austin, 1310 Clay and 5705 Richmond. CK

It always bothers us to find a furniture store with merchandise bunched together without price tags attached. Does that mean the prices change with the stock market or what? We couldn't bear it and said, "Bull!" We had to ask EVERY price! We did see an ANDERSON HICKEY desk for $189.50 (reg. $236.96), steno chairs at $59.50 (reg. $99.50), matching chairs at $139.50 (reg. $169.50) and a 4-drawer legal ANDERSON HICKEY file for $134.50 (reg. $175.80). They also bought and traded. CK

See write-up under "Buying Services." (New Listings Section)

We're gonna file Houston Desk Co. under "U" for Unbelievable savings on desks, chairs and file cabinets. Posture chairs for $87 (reg. $149) kept our backs straight and who wood believe a wood desk for $200? Don't want to refurnish your office? Refinish instead. Houston Desk could strip away the old and put on the new. CK

***
CARROLL DISCOUNT FURNITURE
5012 Bellaire Blvd.
Houston
Tel. 667-6668
M-F 9-5:30/S 10-4

***
THE DESK FACTORY
5705 Richmond
Houston
Tel. 780-7058
M-F 9-6/S 9-4

*
DOLLAR SALES
1901 N. Shepherd
Houston
Tel. 862-4239
M-F 9-6/S 9-5

****
HOUSTON CONSUMER CENTER

****
HOUSTON DESK CO.
2811 Washington Ave.
Houston
Tel. 869-5939
M-F 8:30-5/S 8:30-12

**NR
SOUTHWEST
AUCTION AND
LIQUIDATING CO.**
1275 Pinemont
Houston
Tel. 661-1978
Periodic

Southwest Auction and Liquidating Co. bid us welcome to their not-so-regular auctions. They may have an auction once a week or once a month, depending on what they have accumulated to auction. Clothing, jewelry, restaurant equipment and office furniture could pass over their auction block at any time. Check newspaper for ads or call for time and date. CK, MC, V

ORIENTAL RUGS

*****
**BAGDAD CARPET &
CLEANING CO.**
5869 Westheimer
Houston
Tel. 783-3500
M-F 9-5:30

Savings are in the Bag, dad! Ali Baba and his forty thieves could have furnished their hideout quite classily with Oriental rugs (6' X 9') for $1295. No need to worry about the dew dropping in since they cleaned rugs (9' X 10') Oriental for $81. CK, MC, V

PAPER GOODS AND PARTY SUPPLIES

*****
PAPER, ETC.
8715 Katy Frwy.
Houston
Tel. 465-5137
M-S 9:30-5:30

Paper, etc.
Paper plates, etc.
Styrofoam cups, etc.
Plastic tableware, etc.
Paper bags, etc.
Sell in bulk, etc.
Good prices, etc.
3409 Gulf Freeway, 7441 SW Freeway, etc.
CK, MC, SC, V

****
**TEXAS NOVELTY
COMPANY**
2605 S. Shepherd
Houston
Tel. 528-4961
M-F 9-5/S 9-12

How would you like a collapsed lung? Go to Texas Novelty. We found them selling balloons by the gross for $13.20! Small party toys were $6.60 a gross. Their wide range of party goods were a bit dusty, but the prices were unsneezeable. CK

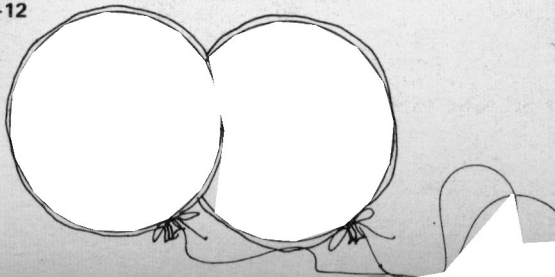

124

PAWN SHOPS

AAA-A Pawn Co. will buy the gold fillings out of your mouth. Also class rings, silver or turquoise. You might find a bargain in the jewelry section, but buyer beware. There's no guarantee if someone else appraises your buy for less than the purchase price. Tuned in on some stereos ranging in price from $50-$300 and turned on some T.V.'s in the $59-$300 price range. $

*
AAA-A PAWN CO.
4402 Airline
Houston
Tel. 697-6020
M-S 10-6

Their diamond prices sounded good. If the quality was good (we're no experts) we would say they were about 50% off. The stereo prices were music to our ears (ELECTROPHONIC for $50) and the supply of tools, lamps and typewriters were more than adequate. CK

***
MONEY UNLIMITED
7102 Long Point
Houston
Tel. 681-1329
M-S 9-6

Morgan the pirate was probably friendlier. We left Morgan's Family Center Pawn Shop as though we were walking a plank. A "no time to chat" sort of business with traditional pawn shop merchandise for sale—including gold jewelry and hand crafted items. We tried to act like kin folk bargainers, but they wanted no relations with us. CK, MC, V

*
MORGAN'S FAMILY CENTER PAWN SHOP
8553 Long Point
Houston
Tel. 467-6235
M-S 9-6

There are a few ahead of the Pac, but not many. We saw a large selection of watches—LAUNGINE, AUSTIN, ELGIN, BULOVA and NEIMAN MARCUS—priced from $35-$100. Our eyes twinkled at a stereo package, consisting of MARANTZ receiver, two SONY speakers, 8-track, SARSUI turntable for $575. You'd have to be pretty lively and quick to turn down a black and white T.V. for $65. $

***
PAC, INC.
4811 Griggs
Houston
Tel. 747-8063
      747-6625
Call for hours

We didn't find the crown jewels, but we did find some stones other than the rolling kind. We weren't tee-d off at WILSON golf clubs (complete set and bag) for $179. Some of the T.V.'s were ADMIRAL but the SEARS color (19") with remote control for $349 ranked higher with us. Also located at 5508 Bellaire Blvd. CK, AE, MC, V

*
ROYAL JEWELRY
7640 Long Point
Houston
Tel. 688-6097
M-S 9-6/F 9-6:30

**
SHAW'S PAWN SHOP
1014 West Gray
Houston
Tel. 522-4884
M-S 9:30-6

It didn't take a pass word to get in here, only an honest face. Security door won't open until store personnel push the button, so don't go away mad if you find a locked door. We got in quickly (O.K., maybe the girl scout uniform was a bit much) and the bargains were plentiful. ZENITH 19" color T.V. for $189, turntables for $20. Their receivers ($80-$300) received us nicely, and their speakers ($15-$400) spoke our language. CK

**
SPRING BRANCH
JEWELRY & LOAN
8715 Long Point
Houston
Tel. 467-2913
M-S 8:30-6

Spring Branch Jewelry and Loan sprung some pretty good buys on us. A DRESSMAKER sewing machine started at $139 and others stitched along for as much as $169. The T.V.'s started coming on to us at $49 for black and white and we didn't write off a SMITH CORONA typewriter for $199. $

PERSONAL SHOPPERS

NR
THE SEEKERS
9014 Roos Road
Houston
Tel. 777-4430
Call for hours

My neighbor has a dozen mangy dogs. I see-curs everywhere. A better Seekers is the one on Roos Road. We decided to let The Seekers do our finding. Their business was finding what we couldn't find ourselves, whether it was a certain silver or china pattern or a gift to tickle Aunt Tillie. Personal and business gift shopping. $25 service charge minimum. $

POTTERY

**
OLD WORLD STORE
I-20 to FM 31 North
Marshall, Texas
Tel. 938-9201
Call for hours

This is one Old World Columbus would never have left. Two potters on duty, turning their classic clay into pitchers, mugs, jugs and pots. A clear buff color with a customary blue stripe or two. For .12 and up, seconds in pottery are available. Actually 15 different stores under one roof, they also handled glassware, wrought iron, silk flowers, baskets, mats and more. Visit Dallas area location in Mesquite at I-20 and Beltline. CK, MC, V

RECORDS AND TAPES

BW'S. Boogie and Woogie? Black and White? Brown and Woot? Who cares. It's prices that count and they had good ones. BW'S Tapes carried used tapes and records. Used and collectors records for sale, with 45's starting at .25. Used albums in excellent condition (FLEETWOOD MAC $2.99) and new records (reg. $4.99) were on sale for $3.99. Large collection of "picture records", originally produced for the industry only, with actual photographic imprints of the super stars imprinted on the entire record. CK, MC, V

BW'S TAPES
1533 Westheimer
Houston
Tel. 528-1942
M-S 11-7

Nothing prickly about this Cactus. Wide aisles and All-American boys and girls for clerks made this one record store you could take your Grandma in. Lots of categories out of the norm—women's music, spoken word, gospel, classical and import. They try to stay very close to wholesale prices. Also located at 10425 South Post Oak and Classic Cactus at 3203 Fondren. CK, MC, V

CACTUS RECORDS AND TAPES
2930 S. Shepherd
Houston
Tel. 526-9272
M-S 10 am-12 midnight

About 20% over wholesale was what evolved here. Just for the record, if manufacturer's list was $8.98, Evolution was selling it for $6.49. Handled rock, country-western, soul and jazz. No charges accepted. They collected pictures of the presidents. Thirty day guarantee on defective records and tapes. Swing on in and see what's going 'round. CK

EVOLUTION
835 Long Point
Houston
Tel. 467-9456
M-F 10-9/S 10-7

Let the record show that manufacturers list their discs at $8.98, while Record Rack sells them for $6.75. Disco was largest selection, but they were very proud of their imports and female vocals records. No credit cards honored. You gotta have green to make their scene. CK

RECORD RACK
3109 S. Shepherd
Houston
Tel. 524-3602
M-S 10-8

RECORDS AND TAPES

***
RECORD EXCHANGE
5208 Bellaire
Houston
Tel. 666-5555
M-S 11-6

If you're into S & M (especially the "M") try listening to a couple of sides of "Mussolini Speeches" for $2.99. This was one store where making exchanges was their business! We gave them four slightly crumpeled dollar bills and forty-four pennies and got Betty Grable singing "Mother Wore Tights". Other records sold for $4.99 or $5.99 compared to list of $7.98. Most expensive collectors album we saw was "BEATLES BUTCHER" for $280. Uncle Fred says he wouldn't pay $280 for the Beatles in person on his front lawn. CK

**
ROBYN'S
WAREHOUSE
10135 Hammerly
Houston
Tel. 932-1938
M-Th 10-9/F-S 10-10

They weren't Robyn us with $5.99 prices that compared to manufacturers list at $7.98. Their sweetest songs were in the rock and roll collection, with country, jazz and soul backing up. Can return if defective within a reasonable length of time. CK, MC, V

NO STAR
SOUND WAREHOUSE
9560 Hempstead Hwy.
Houston
Tel. 686-8826
M-S 10-10

"Do you have . . ." was curtly answered by "If it's not in the bin, we don't have it!" Well, excuse us! His job was to help me, the customer, and not to get huffy when I needed assistance. If this was the only record store in town, we would convert our phonograph to a paperweight. CK, MC, V

RESALE

**
BARGAIN BOX
RESALE STORE
3316 Mt. Vernon
Houston
Tel. 526-7983
M-S 10-2

A Bargain Box could be getting Mohammed Ali to go three rounds for $100. We didn't have to fight for the bargains at this Bargain Box, though. Nothing shrinking about their African violets, except the price—.50-$2. Skis for sale at a down hill price of only $5 and the twin bedspreads were great cover at $10. CK

**
BARGAIN COUNTER
4005 Bellaire
Houston
Tel. 665-1583
M-S 10-4:30

Let's see, now, I believe we counted well over one hundred bargains at Bargain Counter. This resale shop was a real sleeper! Lots of clean merchandise, clearly marked according to size and price. They said they would take the clothes off your back and sell 'em. (On consignment that is.) CK

Resale Shopping Tips

Some resale shops carry new merchandise, too. But the thrill of it all—where resale shops are concerned—is imagining who wore that gown with the bugle beads (and how did it get that INTERESTING tear right over the DIOR label?). You can save yourself some second-hand thoughts, Rose, if you remember a few Resale Rules:

> The smell of mothballs will NOT disappear overnight. (A little baby powder at the seams and pockets will help. Try to convince everyone that your new perfume is NUIT DE NAPTHA.)

> Even Grande Dames sweat. Don't complain if the armpits are stained.

> Generally, anyone may consign merchandise in good condition. Resale shops may sneer at your polyester, but go into ecstasy over the purple wool you wore once but hated later because it made you look like a 5'7" eggplant.

> You get moral points for having the garment you consign cleaned and mended.

***
BAUBLES & BEADS
1955 W. Gray
Houton
Tel. 523-9350
M-S 10-6

We were pleased to find CHARLES JOR-DAN (shoes $38) and FURSTENBURG (dress $32) had taken up residence at Baubles & Beads. Also renting room here were designer dresses, furs, quality sports-wear, plus some new merchandise from stores at the end of seasons. Take them that floral pink and orange dress dear old Aunt May sent you, and they'll sell it on a 50-50% consignment basis. (Well, Sweetie, at least they'll try). Check directory for other locations. CK, MC, V, SC

**
BEP SWITCH RESALE SHOP
FM 1489
Simonton
Tel. 346-1493
S 10-5/Sun 1-5
Call for hours during wk

BEPrepared to save money, 30 miles south of Houston on FM 1093. Clothing for sale ranging from $3-$20; stained glass window, 14" X 24", for $75. They also had a large collection of antiques. CK

**
BETWEEN US
3612 S. Shepherd
Houston
Tel. 527-9989
T-F 10-5:30/S 10-5

Between Us and regular retail prices was about 50%. They may sell only women's clothes, but the guys (LEONARDO, VIC-TOR) were hanging out here just the same. A three piece silk dress by SALVADORE wormed its way into our hearts for $120, and a PUCCI dress for $40 (just Between Us) was enough to start us blowing the dust off our check books. CK, MC

***
BIZ AND BEAUS RESALE
6369 Westheimer
Houston
Tel. 781-1401
M-S 10-6

We tried to give the business to Biz and Beaus. How could we help it, when we saw WRANGLERS for $8, silk blouses for $12, and dresses $8-$100. Their selection of almost-new apparel was cleanly collectible for us poor working girls. Drop in and give 'em some biz—you could wow your beau with a knock out of a buy. CK, AE, MC, SC, V

**
BLUEBIRD CIRCLE SHOP
613 W. Alabama
Houston
Tel. 528-0470
M-F 10-4/S 10-1

This Bluebird feathered our nest with bar-gains. Selling everything from 1780 card-tables ($1000) to cooking utensils, this store's proceeds go to pay for all doctors of Pediatric Neurology at the Bluebird Clinic at Methodist Hospital. That idea sure didn't get on our nerves at all. CK

We found this Charity Guild-y of having a condescending attitude toward us poor, unfortunate, rag-pickin' customers. Filled to the brim with men's, women's, children's clothing and bric-a-brac. Proceeds do go to a worthy cause which makes it worth a look in our book. We only wish that the clerk had not looked so haughtily down her nose at us. CK

*
CHARITY GUILD RESALE SHOP
1203 Lovett
Houston
Tel. 529-0995
M-F 10-2/S 10-3

Cheez, Cottage, we liked what we saw! This restored frame house was cleaner and more organized than the average thrift store and had a varied stock of household goods, glass, china, plus the usual "guess what this is" items. Proceeds go to the Women's Christian Home (for the temporary housing of troubled women). Uncle Fred says they can send their overflow over to his house. CK

**
COTTAGE THRIFT SHOP
301 Hyde Park at Taft
Houston
No phone listed
M-S 9-4

Crown suited us to a royal-T! We saw books for .10-$1, jewelry for .25-$3 and records for $1. Everything in the store was donated, not on consignment. They sell their merchandise for a real queenly cause—a church home for the aged. CK

*
CROWN RESALE SHOP
316 Shepherd Dr.
Houston
Tel. 862-4832
M-S 9:30-4

Hey! Clappa you hands for a designers! We kept applauding until they showed us encore after encore of bring-down-the-house bargains. EVAN PICONE suits for $70, silk blouses for $27 and an ultra suede dress by CHESTER WEINBERG for $120. This store may play before a standing room only crowd before long. CK, MC

*
ENCORE SHOP
2308 Morse
Houston
Tel. 523-8936
M-S 10-5:30

Fashion Hut-two-three-four! March right in for big savings. We spotted dresses for $10-$18, long dresses for $18-$25 and pantsuits for $12-$25. Everything on consignment. $

**
FASHION HUT
1745 W. 34th
Houston
Tel. 682-5651
T-S 10-4

*

THE GLASS ONION
5426 Chimney Rock
Houston
Tel. 668-6087
M-S 10-7

They sure knew their onions. Prices ranged from $1.49-$200 on everything from tee-shirts to sculpture. Lotsa jewelry and macrame. Everything in the store was on consignment and no matter what you buy, you won't leave with bad shoppers breath. CK, MC, V

***

THE GUILD SHOP
2009 Dunlavy
Houston
Tel. 528-5095
M-F 9:30-3:30
S 9:30-4

'Twas only a Guild with a birdie cage ($60). This surprising church resale shop offered a mahogany bookcase for $450 and a pair of tiger face vases for $9. Castoffs from some of Houston's finest made shopping here fun and educational. (Now we know how the other half buys and sells). All consignment goods, and good they were. CK

*

THE JUNKTIQUE PLACE
3000 N. Main
Baytown
Tel. 422-3726
M-S 9-5

Junk teak sounded like a rundown Chinese sailboat. We went on board and discovered a brass plated bed for $200. In the salon we found a teakwood tea cart, with marble top, for $275. Your biggest problem in shopping here will be in separating the good, the bad and the ugly. Used appliances were $3 and up; light fixtures and vases started at $1. Remember, unique doesn't always mean antique. CK

*

LITTLE FLOWER THRIFT SHOP
3603 Washington Ave.
Houston
Tel. 862-0398
M-S 10-2

This little flower was trying hard not to wilt. Offering a "dignified way for those of limited means to provide for themselves" this store was mainly for the shopper afflicted with empty pocketbook. No price tags were on garments, so we had to ask the volunteers for prices on everything. Flea market buyers beware—they will up the price on you unless your disguise is fool proof. $

**

PAULINE PARKER RESALE SHOP
4507 Kelvin
Houston
Tel. 528-1156
Call for hours

We loved the pearls of Pauline. She had a good collection of costume jewelry, starting at $1. Offered no clothes, no real junk. We did hit a nice riff on a saxophone for $45 and set up bar with a liquor set in marble for $20. The only thing perilous about Pauline's is her hours. Better call ahead first. CK

You may feel sandwiched in at Peanut Butter and Jelly, but the bargains bread there are worth the squeeze. Lots of items by PANDORA (sweaters $2-$4). WINNIE THE POOH stuff offered a honey of a deal. TOUGHSKIN jeans $2-$4; an excellent velour dress $14; a chemise LA COSTA tennis dress was $5. CK, MC

***
PEANUT BUTTER AND JELLY, INC.
820 FM 1960 W
Houston
Tel. 440-6771
M-S 10-5

Cousin Ralph got promoted at the construction camp. He is no longer washing dishes, but is now running the trenching machine. From racks to ditches. We went to Rags to Riches and you can, too. Women's LEVIS could be slipped on for $6-$12, and SAKOWITZ and NEIMAN MARCUS dresses were priced halfway between the two "R's". We spotted antiques, old clocks, pictures and needlepoint. The consignment items were on a 90-day contract, marked down after 30 days. CK

RAGS TO RICHES
6512 Del Monte
Houston
Tel. 781-3666
T-S 10:30-6

The Tattery tale was, "Good stuff for about ½ of its original price." Shop here and you're bound to benefit (and so will the mentally retarded). Junior Forum volunteers staff the store, which is filled to the brim with appliances, apparel and accessories. Costume jewelry was .25-$2. For those who liked to tinker, a non-working T.V. for $5 was a heck of a deal. Uncle Fred hasn't worked in years, but I couldn't hope to get $5 for him. $

THE TATTERY
1402 Spencer Hwy.
Pasadena
Tel. 946-0413
M-S 10-4

Tawdry or not Tawdry—that was the question. The answer, we found, was that it didn't matter, due to the glorious bargains. Loads of original goodies. 1910-1930 brass floor lamps rolled along at $75-$245 and crystal dresser trays from $30-$125 were a steal. A little bit cluttered, but worth the search. You may not get your fortune told here, but the money you save could add up! CK, MC, V

TAWDRY SWEET-HEART, GYPSY SAVAGE, AND THE OTHER WOMAN
1507 Indiana
Houston
Tel. 528-0897
T-S 11-5

RESALE

****
**THIS AND THAT
RESALE**
7500 Boone Road
Houston
Tel. 495-0849
M-S 10-6

This and That keeps getting better all the time. What a delightful place. "This" was jewelry and furniture—"That" was old dolls and brass music stands. An old railroad clock for $149 set our wheels to turning and an old piano bench with brass feet for $89 made us want to sit down and play a tune. Barbara Boyle, the owner, was so energetic and friendly we could have stayed forever, just talking about This and That. Second location at 14356 Memorial Drive. CK, MC, V

**
THRIFT SHOP
(St. Christopher's
Episcopal Church)
9013 Long Point
Houston
Tel. 468-9917
M-T, F-S 10-2
Th 10-2, 5-8

You deserved a medal, St. Christopher. Your prices were LOW! All stock was either consignment or donation and the day we were there, you were moving in a load of furniture. Beds, dressers, tables and clothing were already on display, just waiting for some thrifty person to make a thrifty purchase. CK

*
**THE TREASURE
HOUSE**
336 Orleans
Beaumont
Tel. 832-0253
M-S 8-4

Trays're what waiters carry. Treasure is what we're waiting for. Beginners in the treasure hunting game might start here. No gold doubloons, but this well-arranged and orderly store carried clothing for men, women and children, as well as shoes, accessories, books, pictures and toys, etc., all starting at .25. This store was staffed by volunteers from St. Mark's Episcopal Church. CK

RESTAURANT SUPPLIES

*
**GERBER'S
RESTAURANT
SUPPLY**
2222 Pierce
Houston
Tel. 652-2021
M-F 8-5

Gerber's is no baby food for thought. This fantastic melange of metal cookery, dishes, glasses and cutlery is unequaled for its maturity and full-bodied selection. For low prices, visit the Bargain Corner. The rest is fillet of retail. We gurgled over 5,000 nifty items, including unique pots and pans we bet Julia Child has never seen! But if you drove here for a stove, dear, forget it. No major appliances. Don't forget to check out those unusual bar accessories, though. Some of the glasses are priceless (well, almost!) All sales are final so choose with care. CK, MC, V, GERBER'S CHARGE

134

SADDLES

What in the Dale (Evans) are you paying retail for? We saw suede chaps here for $25 and brass collars were just $20. A corral-full of accouterments await your keen eye—everything for the cowgirl/boy or the would-be novice. Are you bare-back in protest of high prices? Make 'em saddle-sore when you buy yours here—they started at just $200. Is this the saddle-savings place, you ask? Roger, Roy. CK

**
AMERICAN SADDLE COMPANY
16120 I-10 East
Channelview
Tel. 452-0784
M-F 8-6/S 8-4

The Rhinestone Cowboy probably outfits here. These duds are studs. There's something for everyone—from the lowliest goat-roper to rodeo royalty. We herd-ed up saddles starting at $200 and outfitted ourselves in every western garb imaginable. Chaps were corraled at just an O.K. $40. We saw English riding equipment, rodeo gear and show paraphernalia. Mind you, it's not rip-snortin' discount they're toutin'; it's selection and quality they're floutin'! CK, DC, MC, V

*
D & D FARM AND RANCH
516 Interstate 10 E
Sequin (on the way to San Antonio)
Tel. 379-7340
M-F 8-6/S 8-5

SCHOOLS: BEAUTY COLLEGES

De price at Delynn makes de folks want to grin. Experience the thrill of having a stranger's fingers running through your hair. Close your eyes and know the magic of deep scalp massage. You've found the answer to costly, haughty hairdressers. These "Learning Technicians" will shampoo, DEP, cut and set your locks, for much less than "retail" stylists. Call for current rates. Wave bye-bye to high hair permanent-ly. Visit also: 10340 Eastex Freeway. CK

*
DELYNN BEAUTY COLLEGE
5126 Richmond
Houston
Tel. 691-9312
Appts. F-S
Specials W, F

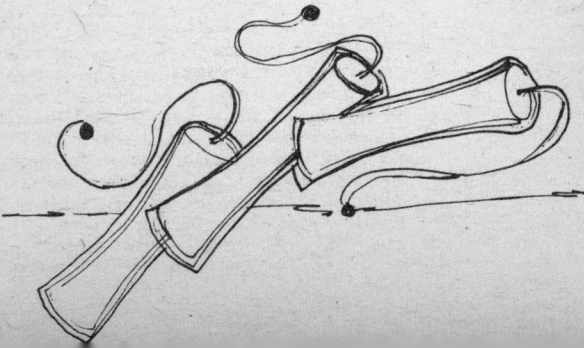

**

BRUCAL'S SHOES
2027 S. Post Oak
Houston
Tel. 621-2991
M-S 9:30-6

Et tu, Brucal? Why is it some discounters view that word (discount) as a pariah? When asked if these are discount prices, this owner was emphatically negative. Yet he did admit their mark-up is a snit compared to retail. So where does one end and two begin? We love ya anyway, Bru, for your sizes 4½-12 women's peddie-pleasers—including a senate full of I. MILLER models. Turn your ides away from Brute-al retail prices. CK, MC, SC, V

*

**CANNON'S
ECONOMY SHOES**
320 Main
Houston
Tel. 226-7182
M-S 8:30-6

Great balls o' fire! These cannon-ball bargains will put you in orbit! We saw shoes starting at $1! We're not saying they're top quality shoes. They aren't. But they ARE shoes! Lots of ORBANOS for men were available. Don't scrutinize too closely and you may come up with something worth (someone's) while. CK

**

**FAL'S WAREHOUSE
OUTLET**
4600 South Main
Houston
Tel. 526-1538
M-S 10-6

Don't fiddle-Fal-dle around. Drop in at this outlet of savings. We saw housewares from $9.95-$24, 4-5 pc. skillets sets for $18.95 and 4-5 pc. TEFLON pans for $18.95. Some sole-ful buys on shoes included men's HUSH PUPPIES for $14.95, kid's JUMPING JACKS for $4, men's and women's ACMES for $14.95-$25 and VERDE for $24.95. PETROCELLI and JAYMAR suits for men were seen. They also feature women's togs. These are closeouts and overruns for the most part. Go to where Pope-ular items are priced in-Fal-ibly. CK, DC, MC, V, AE

*

**FAMOUS BRAND
SHOES**
207 Texas
Baytown
Tel. 427-1514
M-S 9-6

Famous isn't Brand-ing these dogies with hot discounts. They're mostly lukewarm tattoos. We saw HUSH PUPPIES and CALIFORNIA COBBLER, as well as other respected names. But overall, these little leather-ettes were $19-$35. OK, but not cents-sational. They still carry children's shoes but they aren't much to Jump-on, Jack. CK, MC, SC, V

Don't do us any Fayva's fellas. With discount friends like ya'll, who needs retail enemies? Oh, there are some nice brands seen in your racks, but oh, those designing prices! MAYBE one could save a buck here or there (mostly there—at another store). But it's hardly worth the trip for the un-Fayva-ble results. CK, MC, V

½ *
FAYVA SHOES
7549 Westheimer
Westhill Village S.C.
Houston
Tel. 972-9091
M-S 9:30-9

We're Gabby since we hopped-along to this Ranchero del Bargains. Just can't say enough good stuff about these brands for these prices. We saw FASHION CRAFT and BERNARDO brands for women at 60% off retail. Self-serve boxes were stacked neatly in order. Selection was good and the personnel pleasing. This used to be the Vogue Shoe Store Outlet. Be sure to visit. You'll be Hoppy you did! CK, MC, V, SC

****
HOPPER'S SHOES
10066 Long Point
Houston
Tel. 461-6271
M-S 10-6/Th 10-8

In the best National interest, we'd have to say these Brands are defensively priced. We saw men's RED WING'S for $47-$56 and women's BARTOLINI'S for $19. We spotted RED CROSS and NATURALIZERS for a very civil price as well. Keep a look-out for the January and July clearance sales, when you can defend your budget's shoes even better. Visit the warehouse store at 5620 Telephone Road (same prices as other stores). CK, MC, V, SC

**
NATIONAL BRAND SHOES
5312 Airline Dr.
Houston
Tel. 692-5821
M-S 9-8

We picked up on children's POL PARROT, RITE-STEP, KEDS and FLASH DASH. Also saw women's VOGUE and JOLENE and men's STACY ADAMS and CITY CLUB brands. RED WING work boots were working fine at their prices. Lots of soles were going for one-digit figures and those for two-digit were still saved. Let these good ol' boys put a song in your heart. (Twang, Twang). CK, MC, V

***
PICK-N-SAVE SHOE STORE
1600 N. Main St.
Baytown
Tel. 427-1811
M-S 9-6

137

PIX
**

9675 Bissonnet
Houston
Tel. 774-4090
M-S 10-9

Some pedigreed specimens are here, but you have to SEARCH to find the Pix of the litter. NINAS, BERNARDOS, NATURAL-IZERS and JOAN & DAVID were the female critters seen. BOSTONIANS and FREEMANS comprised most of the male offerings. Rack after shelf of not-so-current styles beckon sadly. Prices are appealing if it's not up-to-the-minute you want. Pix is sort of the City Pound of shoe stores. CK, MC, V

SHOES ETC.
**

302 N. Main St.
Dayton
Tel. 258-3361
M-S 8:30-5

Etc., etc., etc.—this Etc. isn't redundant. Ipso facto their bargains make it unique! Save 20-50% on COVER GIRL, VOGUE, MISS BOSTON and CAPRICE women's shoes. Sizes 4-12. Men's work boots—WALKER, WOLVERINE, GEORGIA GIANT and DURANGO—were hard at work saving you dough. All are sent from their other locations. Caveat emptor tho—not every pair is slashed its share. CK, MC, V

THE SHOE HUT
****

4444 W. FM 1960
Houston
Tel. 444-2547
M-F 10-6/S 10-5:30

The natives are restless about the goings-on in this Hut. And well they should be. This frenzied saving activity would rile the blood of the most stoic among us. We discovered ANNE KLEIN, GAROLINI, PAPPAGALLO and PALIZZIO for 50% off original price! The most expensive pair we saw was $22.50! Nifty leather SCOOT SKATES (those shoes with plastic wheels) were offered here. And plenty of $10 pairs were in sized bins throughout the store. Visit deepest, darkest Discount-land; your budget won't be boiled in oil! CK, MC, V

THE SHOE RACK
****

7429 Southwest Frwy.
Houston
Tel. 988-1911
M-S 10-5:30

Go ahead, rack 'em up! You could hit the pocket every time and you'd never get a win like this. These guys are not behind the 8-ball in shoe discounts. They hustle 200 of the 300 brands sold in the USA. And they are all there for 30-50% off! We bought ANDREW GELLER high heels for $55, then found them here for $32! Read it and weep. And if you hit their two monster sales in August and November, you go home with a trophy-full of additional savings. Take the cue from us. If it's bargains on fine shoes you're after, chalk 'em up here! Also, 6528 San Felipe, 11030 Kingspoint. CK, MC, V

This Standard Make never really shifts into second. Men's shoes seen at immoderate retail prices. We observed a range from $22-$125, including DEXTER LOAFERS for $26-$37 and RUDOLPH VALENTINO for $55. STACEY ADAMS was the fairest of the fare. The real and only drawing card here is periodic sales when you can strip their gears and make retail a sin of transmission (transmit $ from their pocket to yours). However, the main office dictates the frequency of these events and their hearts are in reverse. CK, MC, SC, V

*
STANDARD MAKE SHOES
1126 Travis
Houston
Tel. 227-1822

SOUND SYSTEMS

Big savings are Custom-ary at this Center. Stereos (car and home), and portable radios up to 50% off retail. SONY T.V.'s were just 5% above cost! Any equipment for stereo maintenance can be found at lower than retail. The sales help were as friendly as the RCA Victor pup and just as knowledgeable about sound. When it comes to high-fidelity, they'll be true to your budget! CK, DC, MC, V

**
CUSTOM HI-FI DISCOUNT CENTER
2425 S. 11th St.
Beaumont
Tel. 832-2223
M-S 10-6/Th 10-8

See write-up under "Buying Services". (New Listings Section)

****
HOUSTON CONSUMER CENTER

SPORTING GOODS

Don't putter around with golf-awful prices. These Briargrove experts will put you in the driver's seat where you cart home savings on drivers, bags and irons. We saw vinyl bags from $30-$150. Equipment was known by names such as WILSON, RAM, SPAULDING and TITLEIST. Putters ranged from $17-$22 (reg. $35). HOGAN APEX irons were $269 (reg. $400). CK, MC, V

***
BRIARGROVE GOLF CENTER
6161 Westheimer
Houston
Tel. 780-0756
M-F 10-6/S 9-5

★★
CARTER'S COUNTRY
8925 Katy Frwy.
Houston
Tel. 461-1844
M-F 9-9/S 9-6

This Carter doesn't want to disarm. We saw a RUGER .357 caliber for $157 (reg. $180); a REMINGTON MOHAWK was $159; CHARTER ARMS .38 calibers were $111. Don't stop there, however. Check out their entire line of sporting equipment from camouflage shirts to deer lures! We'll be lured back here in the future for our defense mechanisms. CK, MC, V

★
CUT RATE SPORTING GOODS
10553 Telephone
Houston
Tel. 991-5812
M-W 8:30-7
Th-F 8:30-8/S 8:30-6

Troll for savings and cut your rate of sporting goods spending. You can tackle high prices by watching for these weekly ads on fishing goods. That's a specialty here and each week a different brand is on money-saving sale. We saw several brands in stock and the supply sent us reeling. But prices appear close to retail on non-sale items. So watch for your favorite item— then pull in the bargains! CK, V, MC

★★
GOLF TENNIS SPECIALTY CENTER
7639 Westheimer
Houston
Tel. 783-4840
M, Th 10-8/S 9:30-6
T-W, F 10-6

Raise your HEAD and exert your WIL, SON. It doesn't take tremendous effort to beat high prices at their own game. We found a "special items" sale at this center every two weeks that's bound to end that retail racket. Storewide sales sweep the course six times a year. The average tennis racket was $40-$50, with the graphite models going for $220 and the cheapest ones at $20. They offer WILSON, DAVIS, SPAULDING, YAMAHA, HEAD and YON-EX racquets. Test overnight free of charge. CK, MC, SC, V

★★★
PROGOLF DISCOUNTS
9337-A Katy Frwy.
Echo Lane S.C.
Houston
Tel. 932-1707
M-F 10-6/S 9-5/Th 10-8

This golf pro says his prices are "par for the course". They WERE about the same as other discount shops. We saw a FOREPLAY T-shirt for $11.95 (reg. $18). They also offer golf bags, irons and woods in MAC-GREGOR, LYNX, WILSON, FIRST FLIGHT and CONFIDENCE. The discount appears to be about 30% off retail. Don't bogie your golf buys. Stop here for hole-in-one savings. CK, MC, SC, V

You deserve a Sporting chance to save your dough. They'll give it to you here on SHAKESPEARE, PENN, FENWICK, DAIWAN and ZEBCO fishing equipment. We checked out POLICE POSITIVE guns and found them cocked for $202. Lose yourself in a WOOLRICH WILDERNESS shirt for $31. These prices come about via low markup. They seemed very sportsmanlike to us! If you're feeling competitive, take the edge off shopping here. CK, MC, V

**
SPORTING GOODS, INC.
1018 York
Houston
Tel. 222-1421
M-S 8:30-5

This is no chicken Supreme. They're brave enough to knock off a regular 22% from golf clubs and even more on special sales. We saw PRINCE, HEAD, DUNLOP and WILSON rackets for substantial savings, too. A HEAD standard with strings was $35. LA COSTE T-shirts were $16.95 (reg. $21). Check out all their goodies for flavorful savings. CK, MC, V

**
SUPREME GOLF AND TENNIS
4224 San Felipe
Houston
Tel. 626-2440
M-F 10-6/Th 10-8/S 9-5

Don't slide by on a minnow-mum of fishing success. Goldfish were $3.50/lb., worms were $2.08/box and minnows were $2.10/bag. The crayfish are freebies if you wade into the water in front of the store. One clever fellow netted seven gallons worth the day we visited! Worms are fresh from the north daily (as Scarlett O'Hara might say). $

*
TJ BAIT & TACKLE
FM 1960 W. of Dayton
Dayton
Tel. 258-5671
M-F 6-6/S-Sun 6-8

SUNDRIES

Last year's Discount doesn't go as far this year. Smoke-flation took its toll on last year's $4.98/carton price. But at $5.38/carton this year they were still below average (also, .70/package). We were told that REVLON is still 10% off. Beyond that, we couldn't get any info. CK, MC, V

*
DISCOUNT
MED-MART
8802 Long Point
Houston
Tel. 464-5454
M-F 8:30-7/S 8:30-4

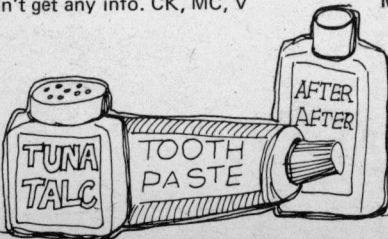

141

SURPLUS AND SALVAGE

*
ACADEMY SURPLUS
5130 Cedar
Houston
Tel. 665-6984
M-S 9-9/Sun 9-6

Savings here may be a moot point. Acrimonious academicians that we are, however, we suggest you visit anyway before stocking up on surplus. The sales help's abruptness needn't preclude savings on camping gear and tents, as well as some out-of-date clothing. Some of this stuff didn't deserve salvaging. But if you're going to ruff-it, no need to pay retail for stuff only you and the bears will see. Nine other locations in the Houston area. CK, MC, V

*
ARON'S DAMAGED FREIGHT
3903 Almeda
Houston
Tel. 529-3901
M-F 9-6/S 9-5

You'll save if you run this Aron before going shopping. We saw BROYHILL, DIXIE, THOMASVILLE, BERNHARDT and MEMPHIS furniture. All were 15-20% off retail. A WEENSTOCK chandelier was $995. Some items were damaged or slightly "scuffed". Little-known brands are housed alongside well-known brothers. Their free delivery within Houston makes this a worthwhile trip to town. CK, MC, V

**
BAYWAY SALVAGE
6800 Bayway
Baytown
No phone listed
M-T, Th-S 9-6

This Salvage-tion army picks up down and out shoppers' spirits. We found furniture pieces of all kinds. Most were from SINGER, BROYHILL and ALLEN MFG. Mattresses were flat cheap. ENGLANDER and WORLD-O-PEDIC were the usual fare. Drop in and drop a coin in your cup of savings. $

*
CENTRAL SALES
5757 Cullen
Houston
Tel. 747-4520
M-F 9-5

There is no Central theme to this hodgepodge melange. A crazy assortment of everything from paper goods to used folding chairs (which sold for $3 each). Paint, store fixtures, racks, file cabinets and refrigerators were discerned in the melee. A G.E. 17 cu. ft. fridge was $315. No telling what you might find here. But we ARE telling it'll be cheaper than retail! CK

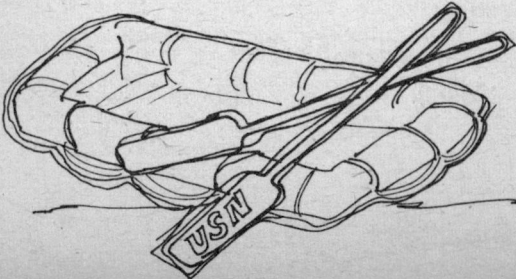

Hey, buddy, wanna a hot tip? They got fenced stuff cheap at the police pound. Like bikes. They got nifty bikes for low-down prices—usually $5-$50. They're sold on the second work day of each month. Come prepared to ride it home or car-rack it (there ain't no delivery in this business, Mac). And speaking of cars, they go twice a year. Watch for auction times and places. Also observed stereos, TV's, radios, camera equipment and other appliances being ripped off for small change. CK

**
CITY OF HOUSTON DEPT. OF SURPLUS AND SALVAGE
5711 Eastex Frwy.
Houston
Tel. 222-3250
M-F 9-3:30

There's nothing disabled about the bargains found here. Used clothing, furniture and appliances were seen in multiples. You can donate your oldies-but-goodies to this tax-deductible worthy cause. Or buy what you see. (Cleverly try to avoid buying back what you donated). There's a small minimum delivery charge. Many veterans of cost-of-living wars shop here. $

*
DISABLED AMERI-CAN VETERANS
104 S. Wayside
Houston
Tel. 923-9181
M-F 8-5/S 8-6

Susan B. goes a little farther at this General Store. We saw modest used clothing with labels cut out. For much less than retail, naturally. Also offered were sundries, cookware, shoes, linens and toys. All were seconds, so they were more affordable than usual. There's not much consistency on prices. $

**
DOLLAR GENERAL STORES
315 N. Main St.
Dayton
Tel. 258-8100
M-S 8:30-5:30

Esther's a tough nut. We couldn't crack her shell for much info. Import-ant items like radios, TV's and stereos were mostly out-of-pawn. Also guns, knives, knuckles and cuffs were observed. Considering the abundance of weaponry around this place, we imagine Esther can back up her cold front! CK, CB, MC, V, DC

*
ESTHER'S IMPORTS
510 Main
Houston
Tel. 227-0762
M-S 9-5

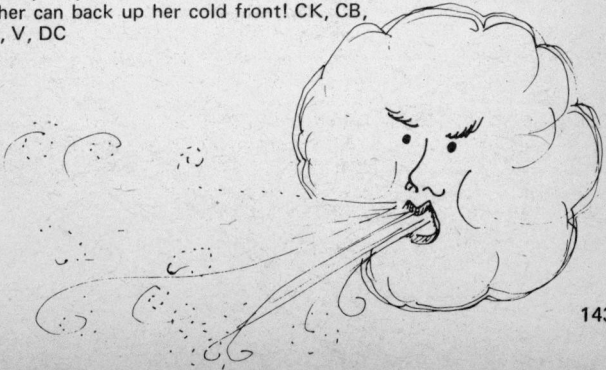

143

*
G.I. SURPLUS
11312-A Old Katy Rd.
Houston
Tel. 493-2432
M-F 10-7/S 9-6

If you've ever known the chagrin of traveling with a child and stopping every 20 minutes for the pause that refreshes, you'll be thrilled to know a port-a-potty was just $6.98 here. It comes with six disposable bags for easy latrine duty. Other essentials seen were leather wine pouches for $3.19 (to help you forget what the kid is doing to the back seat) and sheathed jewel-handled swords for $5.98 (to back up your feigned threats to said kid). Also, first quality DICKIE'S jeans for $11.98, LEVIS for $16.95 and BIG DUDES for $8.97. Visit their third location on Ella Road. CK, MC, V

**
GENSCO
4300 O.S.T. at Cullen
Houston
Tel. 748-3350
M-F 9-5/S 9-2

This store was a candidate for a Mission Impossible assignment when it came to describing their stock. Before our tape self destructed, we saw industrial machinery, fork lifts, buffing wheels, medical supplies, mopeds, diesel engines, generators and paper products. Prices started at $1 and went up. Your mission, should you decide to accept it, is to drop by Gensco and try to find out what they don't have. CK

**
GIANT DISCOUNT CITY
2655 S. 11th
Beaumont
Tel. 842-2240
M-F 9-6

Ever wonder where the Jolly Green Giant got that nifty green suit? Giant Discount City can't claim that fame, but they handled almost every thing else. With seven departments, which included pharmacy, jewelry, hardware, camera, bakery, snack bar and groceries, this store could have you doing all your shopping in one spot. We could have slain high prices with their giant size discounts. CK, MC, V

**
GOODWILL INDUSTRIES
5200 Jensen Dr.
Houston
Tel. 692-6221
M-S 9:30-5:30

Good will toward men, women, and shoppers was over flowing at Goodwill Industries. It was absolute peace on earth to find LEVI'S for .79-$4 and men's suits from $25-$50. Better dresses were hanging around for $7-$25, and we could have slipped on some new shoes for $3.99. This store makes possible many other worthwhile projects sponsored by Goodwill, so any money spent here was doubled in value. CK, MC, V

If you're trying to get back to nature, Gulf Coast Army Navy Surplus can help you make the trip. Lots of camping gear by COLEMAN, including tents, tarps, stoves and lanterns. Their LEVI'S didn't leave us pant-ing $15.95. If you're looking for someplace to keep your pet catfish, drop in. They had plenty of cages for 'em. Six other locations in Houston area. CK, MC, V

*
**GULF COAST ARMY
NAVY SURPLUS**
6423 Bissonnet
Houston
Tel. 774-9836
M-S 9-6

We hit a few lows at Heights Unclaimed Freight but our spirits rose when we saw a used pinball machine for $150. We kept trying to identify that smell in the air and finally discovered English Leather (4 oz. for $4.95). Since we were kinda pooped from all our shopping, we stocked up on vitamins for ½ price. We soon recovered enough to try out a pair of water skis for only $49.95. CK, MC, V

*
**HEIGHTS UN-
CLAIMED FREIGHT**
317 W. 19th
Houston
Tel. 864-8967
M-S 9-5:30

This store didn't need to carry theft insurance. What they had no one would want to steal. Most items had something wrong with them—rips, stains, buttons missing, etc. Maybe some bargains lurking around but watch out for the deductibles. Little girls' T-shirts .97, cotton blouses $2.97, throw rugs $6.97. Maybe they should offer a buyers protection plan! CK

*
**INSURANCE CLAIMS
FIRE SALE CO.**
8151 Long Point
Houston
Tel. 467-7121
M-S 9:30-6

The long play at L & P is their pricing policy. They will let you bargain for something you really love, but don't want to pay an arm and a leg for. Haggle-lujah! 1400 sq. ft. filled with kitchenware, notions, furniture (baby beds $5-$10) and tennis shoes (2000 pairs!). No guarantees that anything will work, but keep digging. You just might find a treasure of a bargain. CK

*
L&P SALES
5100 S. Wayside
Houston
Tel. 641-0555
M-F 9-6/S 9-5:30

This store was not to be confused with the one in New York. Little chance of that happening since this store carried mainly appliances, furniture and decorative (and we use the term loosely) household items. Saw a 14 cu. ft. KELVINATOR refrigerator for $469. Whoopee? MC, V

*
MACY'S
5515 Almeda
Houston
Tel. 528-1297
M-F 10-7/S 10-3

145

*

PURPLE HEART
6632 Harrisburg
Houston
Tel. 921-4131
M-S 9:30-6/F 9:30-9

Purple Heart was not worth getting wounded over. A non-profit organization. You may have visited two of their three locations without even knowing it, since two of them are listed as public telephones! The stores are real though, with cash and carry, no deliveries. They will pick up donations within the city limits. See their other locations at 311 W. 19th Street and 2300 North Main. $

*

**THE SALVAGE CTR.
OF HOUSTON**
5601 Navigation
Houston
Tel. 926-4473
M-S 10-6

Not a bargain hunter's salvation. Everything from deodorant to recliners, but the prices and the quality were not redeeming. Bookshelves for $69, but in our book, that's no bargain. A delivery charge of $15 was a good place for a "stick 'em up" as far as we were concerned. CK

*

SALVATION ARMY
7111 Lawndale
Houston
Tel. 926-0381
M-S 8:30-4:30

We've always heard about army red tape, and the Salvation Army was no different. After spending 30 minutes with 10 different people, we got the following classified info: they will pick up your donations even if you live outside the city limits, but delivery is another thing. They will deliver only on purchases over $50. $5 delivery charge inside the Loop, $10 outside the Loop, and $15 outside the city limits. For truck pick up, call 869-3551. Check directory for other locations.

*

**SURPLUS PRODUCTS
COMPANY**
5720 College
Beaumont
Tel. 866-4568
M-S 9-5:30

We saw more sur-minus than surplus. Rank and file military surplus at only a fair descent from retail. TEX PORT tents for $29.98, plus foot lockers, men's work shoes and boots. From the looks of the store, we thought we'd stumbled into a combat zone. CK, MC, V

*

TIMELY IMPORTS
605 Main
Houston
Tel. 222-2026
M-S 9:30-6

If you don't watch it, Timely Imports just might unwind some seconds on you. Lingerie, linens, decorative knick-knacks, jewelry, radios and televisions were displayed in a sort of here-and-there approach, with nothing out of the ordinary to get us wound up. Oh well, time marches on and so did we. CK, AE, DC, MC, V

This tower was leaning toward retail. Most of the prices we saw there could have been beaten by almost any other store, and the merchandise was more basement than tower in nature. Only worth a trip if you're held at gun point. CK, MC, V

**NO STAR
TOWER BARGAIN
CTR. WAREHOUSE**
Hwy. 35 N
Bay City
Tel. 245-7291
M-S 8-5/Closed 12-1

*
THE WAREHOUSE
1300 Wayside
Houston
Tel. 923-2594
M-F 9-6/S 9-5:30

We could have been canned over their canned goods, lugged some luggage (5-pc. set $97) or gone into therapy on a Queen size THER-A-PEDIC for $139. A 7-pc. TEFLON set was a bit sticky at $19. A bargain or not a bargain was the question, and we'll leave it up to you for the answer. CK, MC, V

NV
**YALLER MOON
DISCOUNT CENTER**
711 Gray
Houston
Tel. 658-9821
M-S 9-5:30

Yaller Moon Discount Center had gone behind a cloud when we stopped by to visit. The store was closed for remodeling. No one seemed to know when the clouds would part and the store would re-open, but from our visit before, we think we'll keep watching for the silver lining, since they stocked everything from panty hose to light bulbs at star bright prices. CK

THRIFT BAKERIES

Since we always knead dough, we love the 20% savings of their day old products. Put 'em in the fridge for a bit and the goods will recapture that just baked taste. Same items as those sold at grocery stores.

11127 Bellaire (495-6243)
915 College (944-9298)
1228 W. 43 (681-3933)
604 W. Mount (447-5046)

**MRS. BAIRD'S
THRIFT STORE**
M-S 9:30-5:30
CK

105 N. 11th, Beaumont (835-8167)
301 Sampson, Houston (222-1927)

**COOKBOOK BREAD
DISCOUNT**
M-S 9-5:30
CK

THRIFT BAKERIES

**RAINBO BAKERY
THRIFT STORE**
M-S 9-5
$

4104 Leeland (237-0001)
1118 Eastex Frwy. (449-7214)
247 E. Crosstimbers (697-4557)
7300 Little York Road W. (466-4166)
3603 Red Bluff (477-4339)
1414 Federal Road (453-8417)
6340 Skyline (789-0560)
9749 Long Point (465-8247)

TOYS

*

FUN CITY TOYS
8300 Gessner
Houston
Tel. 774-6384
M-S 10-9

We toy-ed around with the bargains here and managed to play with a few. STAR WARS DEATH STAR STATION was $21 (reg. $25) and an ENTEX electronic baseball game was a hit at $29 (reg. $44). The savings were not too much fun. Visit other locations at 9345 Katy Freeway and South Loop. CK, MC, V

**

TOYS "R" US
10220 Almeda-Genoa
Houston
Tel. 941-1920
M-S 10-9

This store was a kid's paradise. Toys "R" Us at prices "U" can afford. We kicked around some soccer balls for $10 and started our own Star War at the DEATH STAR STATION for $18.97. Toys, games and baby furniture filled the place to overflowing at prices that didn't require us to autograph too many checks. Made us wish we were kids again. Check directory for other locations. CK, MC, V

TRANSPORTATION

NR
**AAACON AUTO
TRANSPORT, INC.**
1310 Prairie
Houston
Tel. 237-9721
Call for hours

A squirrel would have to move fast to catch this Aaacon. A tried and true way to transport your wheels. With over 85 offices nationwide, you can leave the driving to them. A few weeks' notice is a must and they'll insure your vehicle for up to a million bucks. Houston to San Francisco transport, for example, is about $165, plus gas allowance. $

TROPHIES

They win the cheap award. This is a good place for riding ribbons, trophies and decorative medals. 50% off the continental catalog sales price. Hooray for the winner! CK

***
DISCOUNT TROPHIES, INC.
11040 S. Post Oak
Houston
Tel. 729-1574
M-F 8:30-5:30/S 8-1

T.V.'S

Advance to the rear of the class. About 20% off on mostly ZENITH, complete with guarantee or warranty. Limited selection, but service was with a smile. CK, MC, V

*
ADVANCED COLOR T.V.
11722½ Hempstead
Houston
Tel. 686-5581
M-F 8-5:30/S 9-12

See write-up under "Buying Services." (New Listings Section)

****
HOUSTON CONSUMER CENTER

Why drive to Chicago to see Marshall when you can stay here and visit Stan instead? Fields of bargains on SONY, ZENITH, TOSHIBA, RCA, MAYTAG and KITCHEN-AID. Cost plus 20% on all, along with guarantees and warranties. Repairs done on their own merchandise only. Mrs. S. is the woman in the know and claims an excess of $1 million in business each year. CK

****
STANFIELD'S COLOR T.V. & APPLIANCES
3001-A Fondren
Houston
Tel. 784-0010
M, Th 9-8/T-S 9-5

UNFINISHED FURNITURE

Oak-kay, folks, here 'tis! Furniture Unfinished so you can add your own personal touches. Dining and living room varieties mostly. An antique reproduction chair was just $59, oak tables start at $150 and desks range from $60-$700 for solid oak. Tie a yellow ribbon 'round that oak and cart it home yourself or have it delivered for $15. CK, AE, MC, V, SC

*
HOUSTON UNPAINTED FURNITURE
1640 FM 1960
Houston
Tel. 444-8357
M-F 10-8/S 10-6

UNFINISHED FURNITURE

**
**UNPAINTED
FURNITURE CENTER**
4722 Richmond Ave.
Houston
Tel. 621-4100
T-S 10-6/M, Th 10-9

No pine in the sky, this store offers weekly specials that are hard to knock. Unpainted but not unworthy of your attention. 36" round oak table was $152, an aspen and maplewood pedestal table $59, 4-drawer campaign chest $48. Look for clearance sales on staining supplies and occasional items. CK, MC, V

UNIFORMS

*
**KORNELL
UNIFORMS**
5564 North Frwy.
Houston
Tel. 694-9929
M-S 10-6

We went crackers over their poly blends but combed the racks for cotton. Head up to Northtown for lab coats ($12.98-$20), black serving dresses ($14) and more. 10-30% savings on volume orders. CK, MC, V

*
MEDICAL MART
2405 McFaddin
Beaumont
Tel. 832-3481
M-F 8:30-5:30/S 9-1

With 12 hospitals and clinics in Beaumont, we figured an Rx for uniforms was indicated. CLINIC, MILLER and NURSE MATES brands for men and women. Shoes too. Recommended in large doses. CK, MC, V

*
THE UNIFORM SHOP
1605 N. Pruett
Baytown
Tel. 427-4127
M-F 10-6/S 10-5

Uniformly good prices on high-quality merchandise except in January and July, when they get better. Then look out—it's no holds barred with terrific sales. Sizes range from XS to XL. Cute T-shirts like the one that reads "Marry me and get your nursing care free". MC, V

UPHOLSTERERS

***
**GREEN DOOR
INTERIORS**
2702 Capitol
Houston
Tel. 224-0570
M-F 7:30-6/Th 7:30-9

Behind this Green Door swatch out for the finest re-do's around. Upholstering, drapes, bedspreads . . . even walls, done to your specifications. Mrs. Sullivan may not be the quickest, but she is among the best in town. You might save a bit by purchasing fabric downstairs at Leggett's, then bringing it up for the labor. CK

150

We thought spilling a bottle of Geritol on the couch might give it a lift, but instead it left a big ugly stain. That's when we called in Johnson. Would you believe he picked it up, reupholstered it and delivered it back for a mere $125? Mr. J. also quoted $65 for recovering a living room chair. How could we resist? Please pass the mustard, William. CK

**
JOHNSON'S
UPHOLSTERY
1015 W. 34th
Houston
Tel. 861-5872
Call for hours

USED FURNITURE

This Cort surely was jesting when he claimed the best discounts in town. We entertained a motion to check elsewhere before purchasing a $139 bookcase and $89 contemporary-look chair. Scanty selection on accessories. Don't court disaster by going into the stacked side of the store—doesn't look too safe. CK, MC, V

*
CORT FURNITURE
RENTAL
CLEARANCE
CENTER
8002 Long Point
Houston
Tel. 987-2690
M, Th 10-9/T-W, F 10-7
S 9-6

OK, Corral—the roundup of used hotel furnishings, appliances and office furniture ain't much to chaw over. The philosophy here appears to be "head 'em up, move 'em out". Their stock obviously isn't of the highest breed, but you might find a bargain or two worth shooting about. CK, MC, V

*
FURNITURE
CORRAL, INC.
6807 Telephone Rd.
Houston
Tel. 649-3182
M-F 9-6/S 9-2

WALL COVERINGS

You can Bank on 50% savings on paint and wallpaper. Supplies were limited but the price was right. Paint, wallpaper, various jewelry, brass and old boxes of floor tile were all available, but look before you leap. No allowances for errors that aren't their vault. CK

*
THE BANK
606 Park
Baytown
Tel. 472-9056
M-S 9-5

****
**DISCONTINUED
WALLPAPER CO.**
10902 S. Post Oak
Houston
Tel. 729-7811
M-S 10:30-5

"You'll hang for this" could be their motto since the 40-80% savings offered at this self service wallpaper barn was hard to beat. SCHUMACHER prints (from $5.66/roll) were hanging around just waiting to be bought, and they even had charts to figure your approximate yardage. Quantity purchases bring even further reductions. Foil, vinyl print, solid, geometric hand print, grass cloth and prepaste were all available. Be sure you make the right choice—no refunds or exchanges made. Check directory for other locations. CK

*
**ECONOMY
WALLPAPER AND
PAINT STORE**
2201 Airline
Houston
Tel. 861-5916
M-S 9-5:30

A wallflower of a wallpaper store. Very small selection of inexpensive paper (from .95-$1.90) in flowers, plaids, prints and the usual designs. GULF STATES paint was 20% off. A real Plain Jane of a store. What a bore. CK

*
**GESSNER WALL-
PAPER SHOWROOM**
1507 Gessner
Houston
Tel. 932-9915
M-F 10-6/S 10-2

Anyway, you hang it, savings of 40% looks pretty darn good. Selection is limited to discontinued wallpaper so don't guess at how much you'll need—be sure. GLORIA VANDERBILT wallcoverings and other well known names are full retail but since we weren't too hung up on names, we picked the ones that offered real savings. CK, MC, V

NR
**KEITH & MERDENE
CROSBY**
Northwest Houston
Tel. 445-0412
M-F 8:30-5

Keith and Merdene Crosby would like to help you with your hang ups. Buy your own wallpaper and they'll give your walls a new look. Prices vary according to the kind of paper used and the room size. Usual minimum charge is $35. They service northwest Houston area only, working out of their home. $

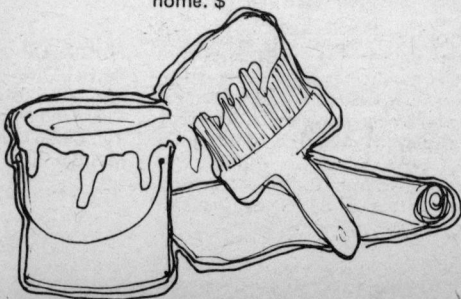

When we told Aunt Tillie that Wallpaper Scrap Yard sold wallpaper by the pound she said she was out of luck since she only had a few lire and a Canadian dime. (Aunt Tillie's always been a bit whacko). We checked her into a good hospital and proceeded to take advantage of the terrific savings on flocks, stripes, solids and geometric wallpaper they had to offer for $1.40 a pound. A few sticky situations—all stock was classified defective, no catalogs all self service, and we had to check carefully as some of the paper was damaged at the ends. No refunds, either. CK

***
WALLPAPER SCRAP YARD
4000-K Airline
Houston
Tel. 691-4400
M-S 10-5:30

Got something you'd like to cover up? Wallpapers To Go had all the answers to our bland wall blues. Sample swatches were conveniently displayed and categorically arranged on mini-walls with maxi aisle room in between. 50-70% off on discontinued items, 20% off first quality. If the only thing you're good at hanging is around, then duck into the back of the store where classes are held to help you turn pro. Twice a year they hold a "Penny Sale" (buy one roll, get the next one for a penny). Check directory for other locations. CK, MC, V

***
WALLPAPERS TO GO
9651 Katy Frwy.
Houston
Tel. 932-1466
M-F 10-9/S 10-6
Sun 12-5

WESTERN WEAR

We galloped into Diamond C Western Wearhouse and found ole high prices had turned tail and run. Offered a full selection of men's and women's western wear and children's sizes three and up. Keep your eyes open and be ready to draw your wallet at the first sight of a bargain. CK, MC, V

**
DIAMOND C WESTERN WEARHOUSE
706 N. Alexander
Baytown
Tel. 427-0733
M-F 9-8/S 9-6

A house may not be a home, but House of Bargains was home to low prices. Sold here at a fraction of their original cost, these were the buys we wanted to move to new surroundings—namely our closets. Loads of garments, displayed anywhere room could be found. WRANGLERS, ACME and WESTERN, in sizes from toddlers to grown-ups. Dresses started at $8.99 and jeans at $10.99. CK, MC, V

**
HOUSE OF BARGAINS
100 W. Houston
Cleveland N. of 17
Tel. 592-8122
M-S 9-5:30

*

**TEX MADE
LEATHERS**
6311 Irvington
Houston
Tel. 695-3351
M-F 8-5

We were saying, "We'll take this and this and this" until we found out we had to have a store and a tax-exemption number in order to get in on the discounts. The public was allowed to take advantage of their so-called "unannounced sales", though, during which a $23 purse might sell for $4. A variety of belts, moccasins and other western style goodies (all seconds) were available. CK, MC, V

****

**THE WESTERN
FAIR**
Main Street
Lott
Tel. (817) 584-3751
M-S 8:30-5:30

Even though this was one fair where we didn't get taken on any rides, our heads were still swimming after we saw all the bargains on westernwear. One block long, with more shoppers and more name brands than we could count. LEE, LEVI'S, TONY LAMA, JUSTIN and many more were all in this corral, just waiting to be cut out of the herd. 50% savings almost started a stampede as we grabbed up some of the best buys and headed back to the ranch. CK

WOMEN'S WEAR

**

ADRIEN'S
666 Memorial City S.C.
Houston
Tel. 468-3641
M-F 10-9/S 10-6

She was not Adrien on our finances. What this store lacked in furnishings, they made up in good prices. Better quality ladies' ready to wear, including JONATHAN LOGAN, BUTTE KNITS and GILBERT. Coats were the best deals in the house; be sure to ask them about the specifics of their layaway plan—no limit on amount or time. CK, AE, MC, SC, V

****

**THE BUTTONWOOD
TREE**
2609 Richmond
Houston
Tel. 523-0527
M-Th 10-7/F-S 10-6

They hit bargains on the button! This was one tree we could prune bargains off all day. They stay open 'til 7, Monday thru Thursday so you can pick up something quick for that spur of the moment big moment. Playtime and weekend clothes in abundance, all 1/3 off and more. High society fashion for skid row prices—a combination that can't be beaten. Ridiculously low sale rack. Purses, jewelry and scarves were available to complete any outfit. Preferred customers always notified of all new arrivals. Ruth, the manager, is still one of our favorites, a real top-of-the-line lady. CK, AE, DC, MC, SC, V

154

Hang your high price clothes woes out to dry at The Clothesline. This sample outlet offered savings of 30-60% on labels like LOUIS CHANEY, NEW FASHION, ROYAL PARK and FIRST EDITION. In sizes 6-10, you're bound to win. CK, MC, V

**
THE CLOTHESLINE
2624 Fondren
Houston
Tel. 782-4941
M-S 10-6

We didn't need St. George to slay the dragon of high prices. This Damsel Inn Dis-Dress handled that job all by herself. Plants, antiques and 1/3 off designer names that took our breath away. Sales staff was the perfect answer to our call for help with our shopping woes. You may also sally forth in the never ending quest for value, at their other location: 1653 Blalock, 461-0026. CK, AE, DC, MC, SC, V

****
THE DAMSEL INN
DIS-DRESS
I-10 at Addicks
600 S. Jackson
Addicks
Tel. 497-2440
M-W 10-6/Th-S 10-9

Dimensions took the Fifth when we tried to find out their percentage of discount. Dresses and sportswear flaunted names like BOBBIE BROOKS, CALVIN KLEIN, ANNE KLEIN, SANFRANCISCAN, FUNNY GIRL, TEA PARTY and FIRST GLANCE. Basically a Junior store, we'll reserve our verdict until all the facts are in. (We can take the Fifth too you know!) Also, 5384 W. 34th and 7619 Westheimer. CK, MC, V

**
DIMENSIONS IN
FASHION
8080 S. Gessner
Houston
Tel. 776-8008
M-F 10-9/S 10-6

The accent was on savings at The Fair Accent Corner. ECCOBAY, PURITAN TRISSI, BOBBIE BROOKS, AILEEN and MR. MARTY all were fair play, with no fouls in the bunch. LEVIS were 20% off so we put some on. Junior sizes 3 and up, misses 6 and up. CK, MC, V

**
THE FAIR ACCENT
CORNER
194 Gateway
Beaumont
Tel. 832-5963
M-W 10-6
Th-S 10-8:30

None of the critters in this barn were branded (all labels were cut) but the variety of the herd was hard to beat. If a dress was reg. $35, they sold it for $19.99. The first markdown after that was $15.99. Received 30-100 cartons of merchandise a week so plenty of new stock was available. Sizes ranged from 3-15 in Juniors, 18½-26½ in half sizes, 6-16 in misses. CK, MC, SC, V

**
FASHION BARN
1408 Richey
Pasadena
Tel. 472-3358
M-F 10-9/S 10-6

½ *
**FASHION FAIR
BOUTIQUE AND
GIFT SHOP**
4556 Griggs
Houston
Tel. 741-9589
M-S 10-7

Small shop with average selection of youthful fashions. LE POUCHE jeans for $25—nothing fair about fashion at that price. $

***
FASHION OUTLET
3915 Spencer Hwy.
Pasadena
Tel. 946-2747
M-S 9-5

We plugged into Fashion Outlet and got a real shock. We gladly let them socket to us when we saw the ½ price bargains. This store will even stay late for customers, if you give 'em a call. Names like ALBERT CAPRARO, NIPON, BUTTE KNITS and ANNE KLEIN were wired in just right to fit our pocket books. Sportswear and dresses sizes 3-22, all at low voltage prices. A real electrifying experience! CK, MC, V

**
FOXY FASHIONS
7968-A Westheimer
Houston
Tel. 781-1571
M-F 10-7/Th 10-9

Quick as a fox we jumped from bargain to bargain. We felt pretty sly to get OUTRAGEOUS, ESTIVO and JOYCE STEVENS for 20% off. The personnel must have thought we had a crafty look, 'cause they seemed a little nervous about answering our questions. Guess they didn't know all bargain hunters have a wild eyed look! CK, MC, SC

**
**ISABEL GERHART'S
BAZAAR SHOP**
5015 Westheimer
Houston
Tel. 626-5500
M-T, F 10-9
W-Th, S 10-6

If Chris Columbus had discovered this place, his Isabel would have gotten her money's worth. This Isabel gave us ours. First rate savings on name brand clothing really rang our chimes. They had three different rooms—Junior Shop, Green Room and Bazaar Shop (this one was filled with designer clothes all year round at discount prices). The sales people could have passed for ex-CIA agents—very close-mouthed. But at those prices, we decided to buy now and ask questions later. MC, V, AE, SC, DC

People are always saying we're Kinda Krazy and we admit we flipped over 30-60% savings. If you are into Juniors (3-13) or Misses (8-18), run—don't walk—to KK. The most delightful place we've seen in years. Brand names like ZENA, HAPPY LEGS, STRAWBERRY PLANT, BOBBIE BROOKS, JANTZEN and KORET OF CALIFORNIA had us hoping for a terminal discount disease. Other locations at 13192 Memorial Drive, 2352 FM 1960 W., 19645 Eastex Freeway, Humble and 21953 E. Katy Freeway in Katy. Also stores in Austin, Dallas, San Antonio and Shreveport. CK, MC, V

****
KINDA KRAZY
7435 Southwest Frwy.
Houston
Tel. 771-0159
M-S 10-6/W 10-8

Lots of double-knit for the not so young at heart. DICKERSON and FOOT SAVER shoes weren't discounted, but well-made separates and dresses were available. Mostly California brands, this store was a drip-dry, wrinkle free heaven. CK, MC, V

*
LADIES DISCOUNT FASHIONS
3922 Westheimer
Houston
Tel. 627-9669
M-S 10-5

We've heard of Loehmann on the totem pole, but this was ridiculous! Usually 50% off on designers like CHRISTIAN DIOR, DIANE VON FURSTENBERG, GIVENCHY and SAKS FIFTH AVENUE. Blouses, shawls, scarves, jeans, dresses, hats, purses and coats. High quality that was so low priced we had to bend over just to read the tags! Fall and Spring showings are held in their back room, each for one day. We'd love to fall in and spring on some of their terrific buys. CK

****
LOEHMANN'S
7455 Southwest Frwy.
Houston
Tel. 777-0164
M-S 10-5:30/W 10-9:30

Don't divorce your husband when he tells you he's been going to Margie's! At this store, he could pick up something really nifty for 30-60% off and bring it on home. This Dallas-based merchandiser (with 40 locations throughout Texas) has a selection of junior and contemporary fashions that will keep any tight fisted husband happy. Some of the labels are cut, but that just makes shopping here more fun. Tell your old man to keep on running around with this lady, and you'll be the mistress of high fashion. CK, MC, SC, V

****
MARGIE'S
Baybrook Mall
Houston
Tel. 986-9787
M-S 10-9

157

***
NAJLA'S
1826 Fountainview
Houston
Tel. 781-6257
M-F 10-6/S 10-6

We nudged Najla up a star (2 * last year). A little low on lighting, but the prices too. CAPRARO, NIPON, CLOVIS RUFFIN, LESLIE FAY and FURSTENBERG were all easy to see, with 25-50% off the retail ticket. Sizes 4-16 were available. Take a flashlight. CK, MC, V, CB, AE

**
NETIA'S LADIES SPORTSWEAR
49 North 11th
Beaumont
Tel. 833-5247
M-S 9:30-5:30

We Netia, Netia! A great place for Beaumonters to become sportily clad. Labels were TRAVELER, NIKKI or LANGTRY. Sizes 3-28. A good selection of quality garments at reasonable prices. CK, MC, V

*
OREM BARGAIN SHOP
4607 W. Orem
Houston
Tel. 433-7538
M-S 10-5

We expected to find the "Pillsbury" label, but didn't. A store where you could buy a dress with one picture of George and get two small miniatures of Honest Abe in return. (That's right folks, .98 dresses!) The specialty of the house was the $5 dress, but selection was warmed over. Visit other location at 107 Avenue F, Stafford. CK

**
PALM BRANCH FASHIONS
5454 North Freeway
Houston
Tel. 694-7198
M-S 10-6/Th 10-8

We stepped into the shade of 40-50% savings under Palm Branch Fashions. A two-step-up junior and misses store with sportswear dresses, some lingerie, in sizes 3-46. Labels like SUNNY SOUTH waved in the breeze, but we weren't too frond of anything we saw. CK, AE, MC, V

*
PIC-A-DILLY
10985 Northwest Frwy.
Houston
Tel. 682-9589
M-S 10-9

We were in a real pickle at Pic-A-Dilly. The Dallas store was kosher, but we did see some SASSON jeans for $15. Worth at least a look, but quality and selection seemed to be limited. Certainly not a Vlasic, but offered a few interesting buys. Beware of the briny buys—such as last season's fashions. CK, MC, V

*
RASPBERRY ROSE
5221 Bellaire Blvd.
Bellaire
Tel. 661-0128
M-F 10-6/S 10-5

This Raspberry Rose tickled us pink with the unusual selection she had to offer. Basically a specialty shop, carrying silk dresses and blouses. Dresses started at $50 and went up to $118. (A bit thorny for our purses). Blouses $28-$36. Her aim was to carry the unusual—nothing prickly about that. CK, MC, V

Marking down the old prices is how they Remark Fashions. They gave us GIVENCHY dresses starting at $24. They vary different sales—one week might have 2 for 1 blouse sale, the next week, 20% off everything. Remarkable! CK, MC, V

***
REMARK FASHIONS
11706 Bellaire Blvd.
Houston
Tel. 498-5089
M-S 10-6

Our INTUITIONS said it was a MINDY MA-LONE we saw, but we flunked the TRIVIA quiz by not recognizing DANIEL CARON. Everything was samples, Junior sizes 7-9, Missy 8-10-12. Discount of 33%. Drop by and decide for yourself if S & S stands for Super Savings or Short and Surly. CK, MC, V

**
S&S SAMPLE SHOP
5209 Bellaire
Bellaire
Tel. 664-2006
M-S 10-5:30
Th 10-7:30

Gave out free samples of friendliness. Four gals who take their business serious and real-ly work at giving top quality service. Savings of 20-35% on labels such as APPLAUSE, STELLA and POGO STICK. Selection and sizes limited, but well displayed and organ-ized. We gave 'em an extra point for their terrific attitudes. CK, MC

**
SAMPLE SHOP
263 . M 1960 W
Houston
Tel. 444-0944
M-S 9:30-5:30

We loved the sample, Simon. Simon said try ANSIE K'S custom clothing for children in the $11-$35 range. BOBBIE BROOKS played along with HOWARD WOLF. Selec-tion for children from size 3, junior size 3 up, and ladies size 8 up. Savings of 70% in off season, samples and overruns. Just be sure to listen for Simon's to say discount clothing. $

***
SIMON'S DISCOUNT CLOTHING
Lucas at Concord
Beaumont
Tel. 892-6341
M-S 9:30-5:30

Simply wonderful describes Simply Fash-ions. The designer names had us running around in circles trying to see them all. MOLLY PARNIS, ALBERT NIPON, FURS-TENBERG, ANNE KLEIN and OSCAR DE LA RENTA were all simply displayed at simply great prices. We simply had to wait though, for their 1/2 of 1/2 price sale. They weren't talking dates—you have to watch the papers for date of sale. Don't take the kids, cause they simply don't allow 'em. Four stars for keeping your rowdy children out. Occasional sales of CHARLES JOURDAN shoes make this store even better. CK, AE, MC, V

****
SIMPLY FASHIONS
4056 Westheimer
Houston
Tel. 621-2662
Sun-F 10-7

WOMEN'S WEAR

*

SOL STEMBLE
1410 Congress
Houston
Tel. 228-1649
W-S 8-3

The stock market has fewer ups and downs than Sol Stemble. Every so often Sol closes his doors, but the sales that precede this are great. Merchandise was displayed in "Dig and Look" style, but the prices made up for the mess. Call for hours, since they vary from week to week. Labels available— CONNIE, NATURALIZER, JANTZEN, CATALINA, HANG TEN, ANNE KLEIN and DIANE VON FURSTENBERG. CK

*

THRIFTY CLEANERS DRESS SHOP
6135 Airline Dr.
Houston
Tel. 695-0327
M-F 7-6/S 8-2

We really cleaned up at Thrifty Cleaners Dress Shop. Great buys on ROUND TWO, JO LESTER, JERRELL and other Texas-made women's wear. Red Tag Sales offer 1/2 off approximately once a month. Don't worry if that just right dress you find has a spot—they can clean it for you right on the spot! CK, MC, V

****

WADIE SALEMEH DRY GOODS
1515 Prairie
Houston
Tel. 224-5699
M-F 9-6:30/S 9-4

Wade in to Wadie Salemeh dry goods and get wet with good buys on BILL BLASS, LEVIS and SAINT CLAIR. Loads of men's suits by BILL BLASS FOR $69 (reg. $240). LEVIS (children's) were 35% off and first quality. We found no Deliah, but some SAMSONITE for 50% off. CK, MC, V

My nephew, the schlemiel, schlepped rotten schmattes down 7th Avenue. He let himself be schmeered, and sold first quality as irregular samples. My schmaltzy wife is the one who made me hire her sister's schmo son. I am a schnook.

(Confused? No need to be. See Underground Shopping Lingo below.

UNDERGROUND SHOPPING LINGO

Like any specialized activity, Underground Shopping has its own language. A little jargon can go a long way toward making you a hit in the fitting rooms and warehouses of the Underground. Here's a list of the most important phrases for your money-spending phases:

AUCTIONS: "In general, (auctions) are for people willing to buy practically anything under the sun at a price they consider a bargain, and the auctioneer considers a profit." Bob Talbert, Detroit Magazine Guide, **Detroit Free Press**

BETTER GARMENTS: More expensive fabrics, better workmanship, exclusivity of design. Better manufacturers usually produce new designs first.

BUDGET GARMENTS: Garments generally produced in volume, using inexpensive or promotional fabrics, and containing little detail or workmanship.

CANCELLATION/As Related to Order: Usually a late delivery returned to manufacturer, who generally disposes of merchandise at a cheaper price. Usually current fashion.

CANCELLATION/Discontinued Style: No longer in production by the manufacturer.

CASH ONLY: Don't be intimidated by this phrase! Credit cards cost YOU a whopping percentage—18% and up—for the convenience of "charging it".

CLOSEOUT: Styles cancelled by the manufacturer, or fashions left unsold at the end of the season.

DESIGNER ORIGINAL SAMPLE: A garment designed and made up as a sample to be shown to buyers, but never produced in quantity for a variety of reasons—didn't sell, fabric unavailable, etc.

DISCOUNT: A certain percentage off suggested retail price. (BEWARE! Just because the word "discount" is part of a store's name, don't assume that their prices are discounted. Many times, the "discount" is anything but!)

DOUBLE KNIT: Fabric knitted with a double stitch on a double needle frame, to provide a double thickness which has the same finish on both sides. Excellent body and stability.

UNDERGROUND SHOPPING LINGO

FACTORY OUTLET: Usually located at the factory, to sell a manufacturer's merchandise directly to the public. The stock usually consists of overruns, store returns, seconds, irregulars, samples and incomplete size ranges. Prices usually low due to the absence of delivery costs, the limitation of credit and the elimination of retail frills.

FIRST QUALITY: No flaws or defects.

HONDLE: Bargain, dicker.

IN SEASON: Current fashion.

IRREGULAR: Containing a minor defect which may or may not affect appearance or wearability. May also be mis-sized, faded dye lot, etc.

JOB LOTS: A large quantity of merchandise acquired at a very low price because the manufacturer wants to dispose of it for a variety of reasons—bankruptcy, fire or smoke damage, closeouts, etc.

JOBBER: One who acts as a middleman between the wholesaler and the retail outlet.

KNOCKOFF: A less expensive copy of an expensive design.

LIQUIDATOR: Often the quickest way (short of a burglary) to get rid of an entire houseful or major collection of merchandise. The liquidator prices, sells and controls traffic in your home or elsewhere for 2-3 days. Of course, there's a fee (usually 25%).

MANUFACTURER'S OUTLET: A location apart from the factory where the manufacturer's goods are sold directly to the public.

MAVEN: An expert; a really knowledgeable person (like your mother).

MILL ENDS AND REMNANTS: Ends of bolts and surplus fabric.

MISH-MOSH: A mess, confusion galore.

MODERATELY-PRICED: Usually a copy of a better manufacturer's successful design—cheaper material; less detail.

OVERRUNS: Manufacturer may have overproduced (by accident or on purpose) a style only to find that he cannot sell it through regular retail channels.

RETAIL: Manufacturer's selling price plus retailer's markup: usually 50 to 60%.

SALESMAN'S SAMPLE: Product prototypes taken on the road by salesmen to be shown to store buyers.

SAMPLE SALES: Time was, news of sample sales traveled by word of mouth, from friend to friend-of-a-friend, or via exclusive mailing lists. Sample shops, sometimes hard to find, are now selling samples directly to the public.

SAMPLE SIZE: Usually the smaller sizes: for women, 7-12; for men, 40 regular in a suit or sportcoat, 32-34 in pants, medium in sportswear. For children, toddler 2, regular 4, children's 7, and preteen 10. Women's shoes 4½-5½, men's 6½-8.

SAMPLES: Before any garment can be mass-produced, samples are made, often by hand, to test the design. After their usefulness is over, they are often sold at a fraction of the original cost. Samples are always ahead of the season, for obvious reasons.

SCHLEMIEL: An unlucky and habitual bungler; dolt.

SCHLEP: To carry clumsily or with difficulty; to lug.

SCHLIMAZEL: An extremely unlucky or inept person; a habitual failure. A schlemiel is a waiter who spills hot soup, and the schlimazel is the one who gets it in his lap.

SCHLOCK: (Rhymes with "crock") Junky-looking, shoddy.

SCHMALTZ: Excessive sentimentality. Excessively profuse flattery or praise.

SCHMATTE: A rag—a housecoat (The garment industry is referred to as The Rag Business, Rag Salesmen or Schmatte Salesmen).

SCHMEER: A bribe.

SCHMO: A dull or stupid person.

SCHMOOSE: To chat idly or gossip.

SCHNAPPS: Strong liquor.

SCHNOOK: A stupid or easily victimized person; a dupe.

SCHNORRER: (Sounds almost like snorer) Compulsive bargain hunter with a negative connotation; person wanting to buy something—practically FREE.

SECOND: Flaws and irregularities more noticeable than in an irregular. There are also "thirds" and "fourths" but these are in need of major repairs.

SUE SPEAKS

It is difficult to describe the taste of a papaya, the aroma of gardenias, the glow of mid-Pacific phosphorescence in moonlight . . . or Sue Goldstein, publisher of **THE UNDERGROUND SHOPPER**. When she speaks before a crowd, multitudinous things happen to the audience. They are amused, informed, entertained, helped, lifted, enriched and maybe just a little shocked.

Sue is close to unique: a feisty, good looking, knowledgeable, consumer oriented businesswoman. She is also a working mother, shopping genius and intense speaker who becomes very nearly evangelical when the subject is saving money.

MS. GOLDSTEIN'S TOP TOPICS

HOW TO BE SUCCESSFUL IN A DRESS, UNLESS YOU'RE A MAN, FOR WHICH THERE IS ANOTHER PLAN.

Sue details the "please do" and "for Heaven's sake, don't" things to be alert for in dressing for ladder climbing.

YOUR MONEY WAS SOMEONE ELSE'S BEFORE IT WAS YOURS.

The Goldstein guide to hanging on to as many of your dollars as possible. The shopping low-down; where to buy in your home town, and how to do it for less.

"HOW'S YOUR TYPING, BABY?" AND OTHER WOMEN IN BUSINESS WAR STORIES.

How to arrive at the top with a clear complexion and conscience. Ms. Goldstein recounts the pitfalls found between the file room and the board room.

Ms. Goldstein has addressed over 1,500 groups, large and small, since she began publishing her bargain shopping guide, **THE UNDERGROUND SHOPPER**, in 1972. Her talks are jam-packed with money-saving information and consumer buying tips, all couched in an entertaining and humorous style, unlike any you have ever heard.

Sue tells her audiences how to find quality merchandise at inexpensive prices, just as she has in the pages of **THE UNDERGROUND SHOPPER**. It has found a place in millions of purses, glove compartments and coat pockets. The message Sue delivers is simple—we do not have to roll over and play dead because of inflation. There are ways for men and women to save substantial amounts of money by shopping wisely.

Sue Goldstein's presentations are highly visual. She is a dynamic delight to see and a positive inspiration to hear. A Sue Goldstein talk is one your group will never forget.

Sue Goldstein is brilliantly flexible. She possesses the ability to spin on the proverbial dime. She can cleverly adapt her speeches to any group or situation, and is a grand master at weaving personal references into the tapestry of her talks.

Her humor is brash, bold, often rib-splitting and ever in good taste.

> *"Pucci? At our house, that's what we call the dog!"*

> *"Bargain pricing doesn't mean giving up quality. We want Robert Redford to pucker, not our zipper facing!"*

> *"Did you know the 'make-ready' charge added to the price of a new automobile is nothing more than a $200 car wash?"*

> *"An appliance is any gadget which has a propensity to fail under stress. I suspect my Congressman is an appliance."*

Sue Goldstein is original and one-of-a-kind. She is both a super businesswoman and consumer advocate. From this unique dual perch, she is able to converse intelligently with folks clustered on both sides of the fence.

For information regarding speaking rates and availability, please call (214) 528-8940 or write us at **SUSANN PUBLICATIONS, INC.**, 3110 North Fitzhugh, Dallas, Texas 75204.

MAIL ORDER

A New Way of Saving

The mail order industry is burgeoning rapidly. There is not much that you can't buy through the mails these days. Everything from appliances to sporting goods is available, and often at great savings. We have listed some great mail order houses that we have found to be faithful purveyors of bargain-priced goods. We suggest you write or call first and ask for a price quote. Furnish them with the brand name and model number.

APPLIANCES

Bondy Export Company
40 Canal St.
New York, NY 10002
(212) 925-7785

PANASONIC, MINOLTA, FARBERWARE, ZENITH and SONY. All kinds of appliances, TV's, stereos, cameras and luggage. They stock a lot of 220 volt for overseas customers.

FOTO ELECTRIC SUPPLY COMPANY
31 Essex St.
New York, NY 10002
(212) 673-5222

Big on SONY (no baloney). Also, KONICA, PANASONIC, ZENITH, VIVITAR, G.E., WESTINGHOUSE and more. Write only—no phone calls for price quotes.

ANTIQUES

BOYNE HOUSE
6 Bridge St.
Kingston, Herfordshire
England, U.K.

Collectible glass and china. Write for catalog.

ART SUPPLIES

PEARL PAINT CO.
308 Canal St.
New York, NY 10013
(212) 431-7932

Everything any budding Rembrandt could ever hope to need, at ridiculously low prices. $50 minimum mail order. Write for catalog.

POLYART PRODUCTS
1199 East 12th St.
Oakland, CA 94606
(415) 451-1048

A good line of acrylic artist's paints and subsidiary supplies, at 50% (and more) off retail. Order by mail and forget about Gogh-ing in your Van.

AUTOMOTIVE

Direct importer of BMW parts. A Capital place to save.

CAPITAL CYCLE
2328 Champlain St. NW
Washington, D.C. 20009
(202) 387-7360

For huge discounts on a big selection of car parts, we pick Cherry's.

CHERRY AUTO PARTS
5650 N. Detroit Ave.
Toledo, Ohio 43612
(419) 476-7222—Ohio residents
(800) 537-8677—Toll free

BOOKS

If you can't Hacker high prices, try Hacker's for your artsy books.

HACKER ART BOOKS
54 West 57th St.
New York, NY 10019
(212) 757-1450

Ask the Marboro man for his free catalog. Book discounts up to 90% off cover price.

MARBORO BOOKS
Mail Order Dept.
205 Moonachie Rd.
Moonachie, NJ 07074
(201) 440-3800

CIGARS

25-50% off on some of the best stogies you ever puffed on.

J-R TOBACCO
108 West 45th St.
New York, NY 10036
(212) 869-8777
(800) 431-2380—Toll free

CLOTHING

If you get drafted again, Call I. Buss. Loads of surplus clothing and camping gear.

I. BUSS AND COMPANY
50 West 17th St.
New York, NY 10011
(212) 242-3338

HY FISHMAN FURS
305 Seventh Ave.
New York, NY 10001
(212) 244-4948

Hy is low. 50% off retail on most of his furs.

SCHACHNER
98 Orchard St.
New York, NY 10002
(212) 674-6910

Feel good all under. Men's, women's and kid's underclothing.

COSMETICS

See **BEAUTIFUL VISIONS**, page 19.

See **ESSENTIAL PRODUCTS**, page 19.

See **HOUSE OF INTERNATIONAL FRAGRANCES**, page. 19.

CRAFTY STUFF

THE HOBBY MARKET
P.O. Box 2172
Fort Worth, TX 76113
(817) 738-2301

30% off on model supplies.

HOLE IN THE WALL
229 E. 14th St.
New York, NY 10003
(212) 533-1350

Jewelry supplies at great savings.

LEATHERCRAFTERS SUPPLY
Mail Order Section
25 Great Jones St.
New York, NY 10012
(212) 673-5460

Up to 40% off on dead animal skins and supplies.

GARDENING

CAPRILAND'S HERB FARM
Silver Street
Coventry, CT 06238
(203) 742-7244

Over 300 kinds of herbs, Herb (plus flowers).

Tulips and other great bulbs.

DUTCH GARDENS
P.O. Box 338
Montvale, NJ 07645
(201) 391-4366

Gardening equipment that snips, cuts, mows down and trims high prices, while it waters and fertilizes savings.

U.S. GENERAL SUPPLY CORP.
100 General Place
Jericho, NY 11753
(516) 333-6655

HOME SUPPLIES

Garbage bags. Sack it for half price.

ABLE PLASTICS
38-15 98th Street
Flushing, NY 11368
(212) 458-0975

Send for their 400-page catalog. You aren't going to believe the stuff they sell.

SARGENT-SOWELL
1185 108th St.
Grand Prairie, Tx 75050
(214) 647-1525

JEWELRY

Remember the old quiz, giveaway shows on TV and radio that promised prizes from Michael C. Fina? Well, there really is one, and he sells watches, clocks, jewelry, china, silverware and more. Send for catalog.

MICHAEL C. FINA
580 Fifth Ave.
New York, NY 10036
(212) 757-2530

LEATHER GOODS

Luggage at lowest prices.

ACE LEATHER PRODUCTS
2211 Avenue "U"
Brooklyn, NY 11229
(212) 891-9713

LINENS

DOWN HOME COMFORTS
P.O. Box 281
West Brattleboro,
Vermont 05301
(802) 348-7944

A comfortable 30% off on pillows.

RUBIN AND GREEN
290 Grand St.
New York, NY 10002
(212) 226-0313

Names like WAMSUTTA, BURLINGTON, MARTEX and SPRINGMAID. Big savings.

MUSICAL

SAM ASH
301 Peninsula Blvd.
Hempstead, NY 11550
(800) 645-3518

Call with brand name and model number for at least 30% savings.

FREEPORT MUSIC
114K Mahan St.
W. Babylon, NY 11704
(516) 643-8081

40% off on names such as LUDWIG, SLINGERLAND and FENDER.

OFFICE STUFF

FRANK EASTERN CO.
625 Broadway
New York, NY 10012
(212) 677-9100

Discounts as high as 60% on a full line of office supplies.

JILOR'S
1178 Broadway
New York, NY 10001
(212) 683-1590

SANYO, SCM, SHARP, CASIO and more. Good savings.

PHOTOGRAPHY

You don't need a degree from Cambridge to buy there. Every conceivable kind of photo equipment, at prices up to 60% off.

CAMBRIDGE CAMERA
Corner 7th Avenue and 13th Street
New York, NY 10011
(212) 675-8600

PRINTING

Havin' trouble Copen with high printing costs? Write for quotes.

COPEN PRESS
100 Berriman St.
Brooklyn, NY 11208
(212) 235-4270

RECORDS

Chesterfield smokes the competition, selling classic, popular, jazz, folk and show tunes at prices up to 60% off.

CHESTERFIELD MUSIC
12 Warren St.
New York, NY 10007
(212) 964-3380

SOUND SYSTEMS

Proudest of their PIONEER, but also stock SANSUI, SEIKO, AKAI, GARRARD, MARANTZ and more.

INTERNATIONAL DISTRIBUTORS
150 West 28th St.
New York, NY 10001
(212) 989-7162

MEDIA RARE

Women In Communications Cookbook

A wackily wonderful collection of celebrity recipes from people famous for most everything except cookery.

* Senator Lloyd Bentsen
* Mrs. William P. Clements
* Greer Garson
* Dorothy Malone
* Stanley Marcus
* Roger Staubach
* Lady Bird Johnson
* Lamar Hunt
* Tom Landry

And many more!

The book is cleverly written and is loaded with extraordinarily scrumptious recipes. This is THE "in" cookbook of the year and no self-respecting kitchen klutz should be without it.

To order, send $6.95 plus $1.50 for postage and handling to:

Celebrity Cookbook
9102 Branch Hollow
Dallas, Texas 75243

TALKING UNDERGROUND

Our representative in Houston, Linda Conner, is THE Underground expert in the Bayou City. From buttons to bows (and arrows) she knows where to buy the best for loads less.

Her experiences shopping in Houston (as our chief researcher) have taken her through most of the outlet stores and bargain back rooms in the city. She is a cut-corner, drag-out-the-discount, haggle-champ shopper who doesn't pay full price for ANYTHING.

Linda has two great kids and a nifty husband, all of whom wear clothes and eat food. Her experience keeping them non-naked and healthy (she is also an R.N.) has added greatly to her expertise as a bargain shopper.

For groups of fifty or more, she will present a bargain shopping speech that will delight any audience interested in saving money on their purchases.

You may call her at (713) 495-7444 or write, care of THE UNDERGROUND SHOPPER, 3110 North Fitzhugh, Dallas, Texas 75204.

RECOMMENDED READING: FREE

SASE—Self Addressed Stamped Envelope

BABYSITTING TIPS

The Pocket Guide to Babysitting (DHD 74-75) is a perfect addition to a sitter's bag of tricks. Write to: U.S. Department of HEW, Washington, D.C. 20201.

If you employ a babysitter, are one, or are a parent of one, this guide is helpful—Sitting Pretty. Send SASE to: Greater N.Y. Safety Council, 302 Fifth Avenue, N.Y., N.Y. 10001.

CONSUMER PUBLICATIONS

Free catalog listing of easy-to-read consumer publications researched and developed by government agencies. Write to: Consumer Information Center, Pueblo, Colorado 81009.

CURRENCY CONVERTER

Free currency converter. Send SASE to Deak-Perara, International Club Building, 1800 K Street N.W., Washington, D.C. 20006.

DUTY FREE

Free booklet telling how much merchandise you can bring home duty free. Write to: U.S. Customs Service, Room 210, 6 World Trade Center, N.Y., N.Y. 10048.

HOW TO SAY, "I'M DYING" . . . ABROAD

If you become ill, or need dental treatment while out of the country, this phrase book is a life-saver. One copy is free by writing: Blue Cross/Blue Shield, Public Relations Department, 233 N. Michigan Avenue, Chicago, IL 60601.

RANCH TOURS

Free directory of ranches to visit. Write to: Dude Ranchers Association, South Laramie, via Tie Siding, Wyoming 82084.

TELEPHONE TIPS

Money saving tips for making your telephone directory more valuable. Write to: Directory Tips, AT&T Room 540, 195 Broadway, N.Y., N.Y. 10017

WILD MUSTANGS

Free wild mustangs from the western states, rounded up by the Bureau of Land Management and WHOA (Wild Horses Organized Assistance). Send for application to: Hilary Wendt, 2521 Old Broadmoor Road; Colorado Springs, Colorado 80906.

WIDOWED

On Being Alone, by Dr. James A. Person, is a wonderful guide for the widowed. Practical advice on all matters of adjustment to the condition of "oneness". Write to: A/M, Department M, 1909 K Street N.W., Washington, D.C. 20049.

RECOMMENDED READING:
To Buy Makes Cents

COMMON SENSE ECONOMICS:
Your Guide to Financial Independence in the Age of Inflation, by John A. Pugsley. Slick hardback. Complicated stuff. Best chapter on insurance, how to buy it. Dated material on premium costs. Common Sense Press, 2232 S.E. Bristol, Suite 208, Santa Ana, California 92707 $10

1979 CONSUMER BUYING GUIDE. Consumer guide published annually, containing prices on almost 10,000 nationally advertised products. Available in bookstores and newsstands.

CONSUMER COMPLAINT GUIDE, by Joseph Rosenbloom. How to go to the top with your complaints. Lists manufacturers of consumer products, complete with name, address and phone number of person to contact.

CONSUMER GUIDE TO LIFE INSURANCE, by J. Tracy Oehlbeck. An intelligent and informative guide to buying and using insurance. Clear explanation of terms will help you read and understand the small print.

CONSUMER SURVIVAL BOOK: How to Fight Inflation, by Marvin L. Bittinger. Workbook layout—fun to read, easy to use.

COOKBOOKS 1 and 2, by Gloria Pitzer, P.O. Box 152, St. Clair, Mich. 79048. Secret restaurant recipes from the fast-food giants, including "Kernel's Fried Chicken", "Hopeless Twinkle Filling" and "Walled-Off Historia Mushroom Beef".

RECOMMENDED READING: To Buy Makes Cents

ENERGY CRISIS SURVIVAL KIT, by Susan Know, Manor Books. From how to dress to stay warm to how not to waste in the bathroom. Easy reading; easy to follow and save.

FORMULA BOOKS 1 and 2, by Norman Stark. How to make countless everyday products from deodorant to detergent. Save as much as 50%.

GREAT GADGET CATALOGUE, by Tania Grossinger. Strange-sounding gadgets with strange-sounding names, yet the most practical items invented are described, located and priced in this book.

HELP: THE USEFUL ALMANAC, Arthur E. Roscose, Ed. How to get help from federal agencies; lists of recalled autos; how to get action; most livable cities.

HOW TO GET GOOD AND HONEST AUTO SERVICE, by Albert Lee. Warner Paperback. Handy paperback guide to choosing the right repair shop, how to spot a repair bandit, how to complain and to whom, how to make sure you don't overpay. Excellent section on symptons and their probable causes.

HOW TO LIVE CHEAP BUT GOOD, by Martin Poriss. Oriented toward doing-it-yourself and saving. Complete with drawings for simple plumbing and electrical repairs.

HOW TO LIVE RICH WHEN YOU'RE NOT, by Rebecca Greer. Innumerable and ingenious tips on stretching your money for travel, food and clothes.

THE INTELLIGENT CONSUMER, Christopher and Bonnie Weathersbee. The environmentalist's approach to thoughtful purchasing of everything from paper plates to houses.

LIFE WITH WORKING PARENTS:
PRACTICAL HINTS FOR EVERYDAY SITUATIONS, by Ester Hautzig. Written for kids 12 and up. Recipes, emergencies, saving and earning money, self-reliance and rainy day suggestions.

MONEY BOOK, by Sylvia Porter. How to earn it, spend it, save it, invest it, borrow it—and use it to better your life.

NATURE GUIDE. Listing of several thousand nature lovers in North America who will usually show visitors beauty spots in their area free of charge. If you notify them in advance, they will not only tell you the best places to go, but may also guide you as well. For this directory, spend $1.30 to Tahoma Audubon Society at 34915 Fourth Avenue South, Federal Way, Washington 98003.

1001 VALUABLE THINGS YOU CAN GET FREE, by Mort Weisinger. Bantam Books. A treasure chest of valuable merchandise (and some not so valuable), offers opportunities and entertainment. Invest in the book, get everything else FREE, from free cookbooks for dieters to a hurricane tracking chart, free calendars to stain removal charts.

THE SAFE FOOD GUIDE, by Barbara DeDuc. Over 3000 brand name foods free of artificial flavoring and coloring listed. Next edition will include foods without preservatives.

THE SUPERMARKET HANDBOOK, by Nikki and David Goldbeck. Comprehensive dissection of the supermarket shelves and bins, focusing in on manufacturers' distorted claims, nutrition, additives, proper selection, storage and preparation of various food items.

THE SUPERMARKET SURVIVAL MANUAL, by Judy Lunn Kemp. Strip the green leaves atop the pineapple so you'll never pay for additional weight! Forget being impressed with fancy words like premium—it costs! Sometimes large eggs are cheaper than small ones. Why pay extra to have cheese sliced for you? These tips and lots more from a survivor of the soaring food costs. Hilarious and practical—money saving the Kemp way.

THE WHOLE KIDS CATALOG, by Peter Cardozo. A book that's alive with interests for the active child—everything from recipes to crafts, puzzles and collecting. A source book, an activity book, and a guide to free things.

THE WOMAN'S GUIDE TO STARTING A BUSINESS, by Claudia Jessup and Genie Chipps. Not for women only, by any means. First part deals with the beginning mechanics of a business. The second part deals with case histories of actual women who are currently making it in the business world.

HOW TO GET ALONG WITH YOUR LAWYER (and Save Money at the Same Time)
by John A. Waller
$9.75

A practicing attorney in Texas for over 20 years tells how to get the best possible legal representation for the least amount of money. Waller outlines how lawyers set fees, how to choose a lawyer, how to negotiate fee arrangements, how to keep legal fees to a minimum. John Waller served on one of the Grievance Committees of the State Bar of Texas . . . so he knows how clients feel about lawyers—and vice versa! He has written an invaluable book for anyone who needs a "friend in court".

WILL KIT
by John A. Waller
$10/$20

Attorney John Waller has produced a serious will kit which will allow you to do it your way—legally. The WILL KIT has everything you need to save yourself from the double bind of high lawyer's fees and estate-gobbling probate laws. Forms and instructions are in easy-to-understand language, minus the legal baffle-gab. Every possible situation is covered, from legacies to the question of "Who raises the kids?" The WILL KIT tells you how to handle life insurance, how to list your assets and more. It's available in 2 forms: the BASIC WILL KIT, which covers everything except unusual bequests or trust provisions, and the REGULAR WILL KIT, which includes everything. BASIC WILL KIT costs $12.50 for 2 persons or $10 for 1; REGULAR WILL KIT costs $20 for 2 persons, $17.50 for 1. The WILL KIT is valid in all states EXCEPT LOUISIANA, and comes with a 30-day return policy.

After examining the less expensive do-it-yourself will packages on the market, we think the WILL KIT is the top of the line. The lawyers on our review committee agree.

THE GOOD IDEAS HOW TO SAVE MONEY BOOK
by Peggy Whitt
$8.45

Hundreds of ways that you can save substantial sums by doing almost everything yourself. Tells you how-to-do-it in laywomen's terms. Illustrated.

Don't pay some guy thousands to build your tennis court, when you can do it yourself for much, much less. Save the extra money for lessons or for a doctor to cure your tennis elbow.

HOW TO BUILD TENNIS COURTS
by S. Blackwell Duncan
$6.45

Redoing your kitchen? Here's a book that can save you a bundle on cabinetry. Easily understood text clearly shows you step-by-step procedures for building your own. No guarantee you won't smash your thumb with your hammer, though.

BUILT-IT BOOK OF CABINETS AND BUILT-INS
by Percy W. Blandford
$9.45

There is nothing around the house that a woman can't do as well as a man. Let this book show you how.

THE HOUSEWIFE HANDYPERSON
by Jacqueline Peake
$6.45

You don't have to have a stained thumb to do a good job repairing and refinishing furniture. All you need is Percy's book.

DO-IT-YOURSELF GUIDE TO FURNITURE REPAIR AND REFINISHING
by Percy W. Blandford
$7.45

If you have ever taken the back off your TV set and been shocked by what you saw, you need this book. Not for klutzes or dummies.

COLOR TV TROUBLE FACT BOOK— PROBLEMS AND SOLUTIONS— FOURTH EDITION
by The Editorial Staff of Electronic Technician/Dealer Magazine
$9.45

The best arts and crafts catalog we've ever seen. Lists hundreds of artisans, with their addresses. Illustrated. The catalog enables you to order unique items directly from the source, at savings of 50% or more.

THE GOODFELLOW CATALOG OF WONDERFUL THINGS
by Christopher Weills
$10.20

A very comprehensive listing of hundreds of flea market items and their current prices. Don't find yourself in a depression because you paid too much for your depression glass.

THE FLEA MARKET PRICE GUIDE
$8.45

MONEY-SAVING BOOKS

We recommend all of the MONEY SAVING BOOKS. To order, see below.

. . . . . $9.45	Built-It Book of Cabinets and Built-Ins
. . . . . $9.45	Color TV Trouble Fact Book
. . . . . $7.45	Do It Yourself Guide to Furniture Repair and Refinishing
. . . . . $8.45	The Flea Market Price Guide
. . . . . $8.45	The Good Ideas How to Save Money Book
. . . . . $10.20	The Goodfellow Catalog of Wonderful Things
. . . . . $6.45	The Housewife Handyperson
. . . . . $6.45	How to Build Tennis Courts
. . . . . $9.75*	How to Get Along With Your Lawyer
. . . . . $10.00*	Will Kit: Basic (1-person, no trust provisions)
. . . . . $12.50*	Will Kit: Basic (2-person, no trust provisions)
. . . . . $17.50*	Will Kit: Regular (1-person, comprehensive)
. . . . . $20.00*	Will Kit: Regular (2-person, comprehensive)

* Texas residents add 5% sales tax

MULTIPLE ORDERS WILL ARRIVE UNDER SEPARATE COVER

Mail Books to:

NAME . . . .

ADDRESS . . . .

CITY . . . . .STATE . . . . .ZIP . . . .

TOTAL AMOUNT ENCLOSED: $. . . . .

Mail To:

The Underground Shopper, 3110 N. Fitzhugh, Dallas, TX 75204

The Underground Shopper

YOU CAN GET YOUR UNDERGROUND SHOPPER
BY MAIL

Traveling to another city? The current editions of **THE UNDER-GROUND SHOPPER** are available for the following cities:

. . . . . $5.50	Dallas/Fort Worth
. . . . . $4.00	Detroit
. . . . . $5.50	Houston
. . . . . $6.50	New York
. . . . . $5.50	San Antonio/Austin

Currently being revised and updated: Atlanta, Boston, Minneapolis/St. Paul, Oklahoma City/Tulsa, San Francisco, Southeast Florida (to include Miami and Fort Lauderdale) and St. Louis.

Watch for **THE UNDERGROUND SHOPPER** in Denver, Kansas City, Los Angeles, New Orleans, Philadelphia, Phoenix, Chicago, Cleveland, Washington, D.C. and Hawaii.

Mail **THE UNDERGROUND SHOPPER** To:

NAME . . . .

ADDRESS . . . .

CITY . . . . .STATE . . . . .ZIP . . . .

TOTAL AMOUNT ENCLOSED: $. . . . .

Mail To:

The Underground Shopper, 3110 N. Fitzhugh, Dallas, TX 75204

CAVIAR EMPTOR—let the eater beware! Is it the good turtle soup, or is it merely mock? Whether you are dining in Granada or Asbury Park, Truth in Menu by Robert N. Hills will keep you from swallowing (and paying for) the lies on the menu. Common menu and food advertising frauds are exposed in this booklet, which covers everything from the Great Bibb Lettuce Robbery to the infamous Roquefortgage. Truth in Menu is available from Hills Communications, 4750 Chevy Chase Drive, Chevy Chase, MD 20015. Cost $1.00.

SERVICES

SusAnn Publications, Inc., 3110 N. Fitzhugh, Dallas, Texas 75204, (214) 528-8940, offers all of the following services:

PUBLISHING CONSULTATION:

The experts at SusAnn Publications work with aspiring authors, helping them each step of the way, from initial manuscript evaluation to final printing and distribution. Call for rates.

GHOST WRITING:

Our staff of writers are adept at producing written material on any subject, in any vein. From humorous speeches to lengthy tomes, love notes to complaints, we can help in telling any story. Call us.

SAY, HAVEN'T WE MET SOMEPLACE?

No? I could have sworn . . . Won't you sit down? Swell! Here, you can put your bag on this chair . . . Care for a drink? . . . Oh, I see . . . Well, neither do I. Waiter! Two iced teas, please . . . May I ask you something . . . rather personal? Yes? Gee, thanks!

Is this your first copy of **THE UNDERGROUND SHOPPER?** Yes. . . . . No. . . . .

If not, when was the last year you bought the **SHOPPER?** . . . .
. . . .

Where did you buy your copy? . . . .

Is there any category of merchandise which we missed that you would like to see included? . . . .

What local shops did we miss that you consider super special? . . . . . .

What local shops claim to offer bargains, but don't? . . . .
. . . .

Have you had any trouble with any of the merchants listed in the book? If so, please tell us about it . . . .
. . . .

Tell us about any pleasant experience you may have had with an **UNDERGROUND SHOPPER** merchant . . . .
. . . .
. . . .

Would you be interested in working part-time for **THE UNDER-GROUND SHOPPER?** Yes. . . . . No. . . . .

Gosh, I sure have enjoyed our conversation. You know so much about so many things . . . I don't suppose you would like to come up to my place for a little while . . . Well, maybe some other time. Where can I write you?

NAME . . . .

ADDRESS. . . . .

CITY . . . . STATE . . . . ZIP . . . .

TELEPHONE . . . .

Thanks . . . Where can you write me? Here's my card.

THE UNDERGROUND SHOPPER, 3110 N. Fitzhugh, Dallas, TX 75204

I hope you'll write . . . I . . . need you.

ALPHABETICAL INDEX

ALPHABETICAL INDEX